PENGUIN BOOKS

summertime

Food by Rodney Greaves
Food photography by Jacqui Blanchard

Bacon and Egg Salad with Chive Mayonnaise

Serves 4

Ingredients

8 slices streaky bacon
6 small eggs, hard-boiled and peeled
3 tomatoes, sliced
1 avocado, peeled and sliced
salad leaves
1 cup croutons

Chive Mayonnaise
125 ml (½ cup) store-bought mayonnaise
2 tbsp fresh chopped chives
salt and pepper

Preheat oven to 200°C.
Place bacon on a baking tray. Cook for approximately 10 minutes, or until crisp.
Meanwhile, make the Chive Mayonnaise.
Cut eggs in half.
Cut each bacon slice into 3.

To make the Chive Mayonnaise
Combine mayonnaise with chives. Season with salt and pepper to taste.

Assembly

Divide eggs, tomato, avocado and salad leaves between 4 plates. Top with a dollop of Chive Mayonnaise. Divide bacon and croutons between the plates and serve.

Scrambled Eggs, Smoked Salmon and Asparagus with Wholegrain Bread

Serves 4

Ingredients

16 fresh asparagus spears
200 g butter, softened
4 slices wholegrain bread
8 eggs, lightly beaten
125 ml (½ cup) cream
¼ cup finely chopped chives
salt and cracked black pepper
8 slices smoked salmon

Preheat oven to 150°C.

Cook asparagus in boiling, salted water for 3 minutes. Drain. Toss in 2 tbsp butter. Place in oven to keep warm.

Lightly toast bread, then butter it. Place in oven to keep warm.

Heat 2 tbsp butter in a large frying pan or saucepan until it begins to bubble. Add eggs, stirring constantly until set.

Add cream and chives and cook until reset and creamy. Season with salt and pepper to taste.

Assembly

Place 1 slice of toast on each plate with 4 asparagus spears. Divide the scrambled eggs between each plate. Top with 2 slices of smoked salmon and serve.

Asparagus spears have tough ends that have to be removed before cooking. Bend the asparagus at the base so that the tough bit snaps off. Trim end with knife before cooking.

Corn Fritters with Spiced Bean and Avocado Salad

Serves 4, makes 12 fritters

Ingredients

Corn Fritters

½ cup flour
¼ tsp baking powder
3 eggs, lightly beaten
1 tbsp milk
2½ cups corn kernels, cooked and well drained
¼ cup finely sliced spring onion
2 tbsp chopped parsley
salt and pepper
vegetable oil for cooking

Spiced Bean and Avocado Salad

12 round green beans, halved
4 tbsp vegetable oil
1 fresh red chilli, deseeded and finely chopped
2 tbsp roughly chopped coriander
1 small red onion, finely sliced
1 x 400-g can cooked white beans, rinsed and drained
1 avocado, peeled and sliced
salt and pepper

To make the Corn Fritters

Whisk the first 4 ingredients together to form a smooth, thick batter. Add corn, spring onion and parsley and mix well. Season with salt and pepper to taste.

Heat a little oil in a large frying pan on a medium to high heat. Spoon 2 tbsp of fritter mix per fritter into frying pan. Cook for 2–3 minutes on each side until golden brown.

To make the Spiced Bean and Avocado Salad

Cook green beans in boiling, salted water for 30 seconds.

Drain and place in cold water to stop them cooking and maintain their colour. Drain when cold. Mix the oil, chilli, coriander and onion in a bowl.

Add the green beans, white beans and avocado. Mix gently.

Season with salt and pepper to taste.

Assembly

Divide the salad between 4 plates. Place 3 fritters on each plate and serve.

To prepare fresh corn kernels, remove the husk from the corn cob and the stringy silk. Cut in half. Stand on its end and cut down each side, removing kernels. Cook in boiling salted water for 2 minutes. Strain and cool under cold running water. Drain.

BRUNCH

Corned Beef Hash Cakes, Poached Egg and Hollandaise Sauce

Serves 6

Ingredients

300 g corned beef, cooked and sliced
5 cups boiled and grated Agria potatoes
½ cup finely chopped spring onion
¼ cup chopped parsley
salt and pepper
flour to shape patties
2 tbsp canola oil
6 eggs, poached
2 tbsp chopped chives
freshly ground black pepper

Hollandaise Sauce
3 egg yolks
1 tbsp white wine vinegar
2 tbsp lemon juice
1 tbsp sugar
200 ml melted butter (hot, not boiling)
salt and pepper

Chop corn beef to a fine dice.

Place in a bowl with the potato, spring onion and parsley. Mix well. Season with salt and pepper to taste.

Dip hands in flour and shape mixture into 6 patties. Heat oil in a large frying pan to a medium to hot heat. Cook the patties until golden brown, approximately 3 minutes each side. Set aside and keep warm.

Meanwhile, poach the eggs and make the Hollandaise Sauce.

To make the Hollandaise Sauce

Place egg yolks, vinegar, lemon juice and sugar in a food processor or bowl.

Process or whisk until pale in colour. Slowly pour in the melted butter until it forms a thick sauce. Season with salt and pepper to taste. Keep in a warm place.

Assembly

Top each pattie with a poached egg. Coat with Hollandaise Sauce. Sprinkle with chives and black pepper. Serve immediately.

Garlic Prawn Roll

Serves 4

Ingredients

4 long, crusty bread rolls
soft butter
1 avocado, peeled, cut into quarters and sliced
2 large tomatoes, cut in half lengthways and sliced
60 ml (¼ cup) canola oil
3 cloves garlic, peeled and thinly sliced
20 raw prawn cutlets, tails removed
salt and pepper
1 tbsp parsley, chopped

Garlic Mayonnaise

125 ml (½ cup) store-bought mayonnaise
2 tbsp tomato sauce
1–2 cloves garlic, finely chopped
salt and pepper

Make the Garlic Mayonnaise and set aside.
Cut bread rolls in half lengthways. Butter lightly. Spread with Garlic Mayonnaise.
Arrange avocado and tomato alternately on the base of the rolls.
Heat canola oil in a frying pan. Cook garlic until golden brown. Remove garlic from the oil.
Reheat the oil in the frying pan. Add the prawns. Season with salt and pepper. Cook for approximately 1 minute on each side.
Place prawns on the roll bases. Sprinkle with garlic slices and chopped parsley. Place top on roll.

To make the Garlic Mayonnaise

Mix mayonnaise and tomato sauce together. Add garlic. Season with salt and pepper to taste.

Mussel and Courgette Fritters

Serves 8, makes approximately 24 fritters

Ingredients

½ cup flour
½ tsp baking powder
5 eggs
24 mussels, cooked and tongues removed
3 courgettes, grated
2–3 cloves garlic, finely chopped
1 cup chopped parsley
salt and pepper
250ml (1 cup) canola oil

Tartare sauce

250 ml (1 cup) store-bought, thick, egg- based mayonnaise
2 medium gherkins, finely chopped
2 tbsp finely chopped capers
2 tbsp finely chopped parsley
salt and pepper

In a bowl, whisk together flour, baking powder and eggs to make a smooth batter.
Cut each mussel into 3. Place in a large bowl.
Place grated courgette on a clean tea-towel. Squeeze out the excess liquid.
Add the mussels, courgette, garlic and parsley to the batter. Mix well. Season with salt and pepper to taste.
Heat oil in a large frying pan to a medium to hot heat. If using a barbecue, brush the flat top with oil.
Spoon mixture, 2 tbsp per fritter, into frying pan, or onto flat top of barbecue. Cook until golden brown on each side.
Serve with tartare sauce, bread or rolls and cold beer.

To make the Tartare Sauce

Mix together mayonnaise, gherkins, capers and parsley. Season with salt and pepper to taste.

Open Asparagus and Egg Sandwich with Caper Butter and Parmesan

Serves 4

Ingredients

24 fresh asparagus spears
2 large bread rolls, cut in half
300 g soft butter
4 eggs
½ cup capers
salad leaves
1 cup shaved Parmesan
2 tbsp chopped flat-leaf parsley

Preheat oven to 180°C.
Bring a saucepan of salted water to the boil. Add asparagus and boil for 3 minutes. Drain. Place asparagus in cold water and when cool, drain well. Brush rolls with 50 g butter and bake in oven until golden brown.
Fry the eggs in 50 g butter and set aside.
Melt 200 g butter in a separate frying pan. Add the asparagus and capers and heat through.

Assembly

Place 2 bread roll halves on each plate. Divide salad leaves between each roll. Place heated asparagus on top of salad leaves and top with a fried egg. Drizzle capers and butter over sandwich. Sprinkle with shaved Parmesan and chopped parsley and serve.

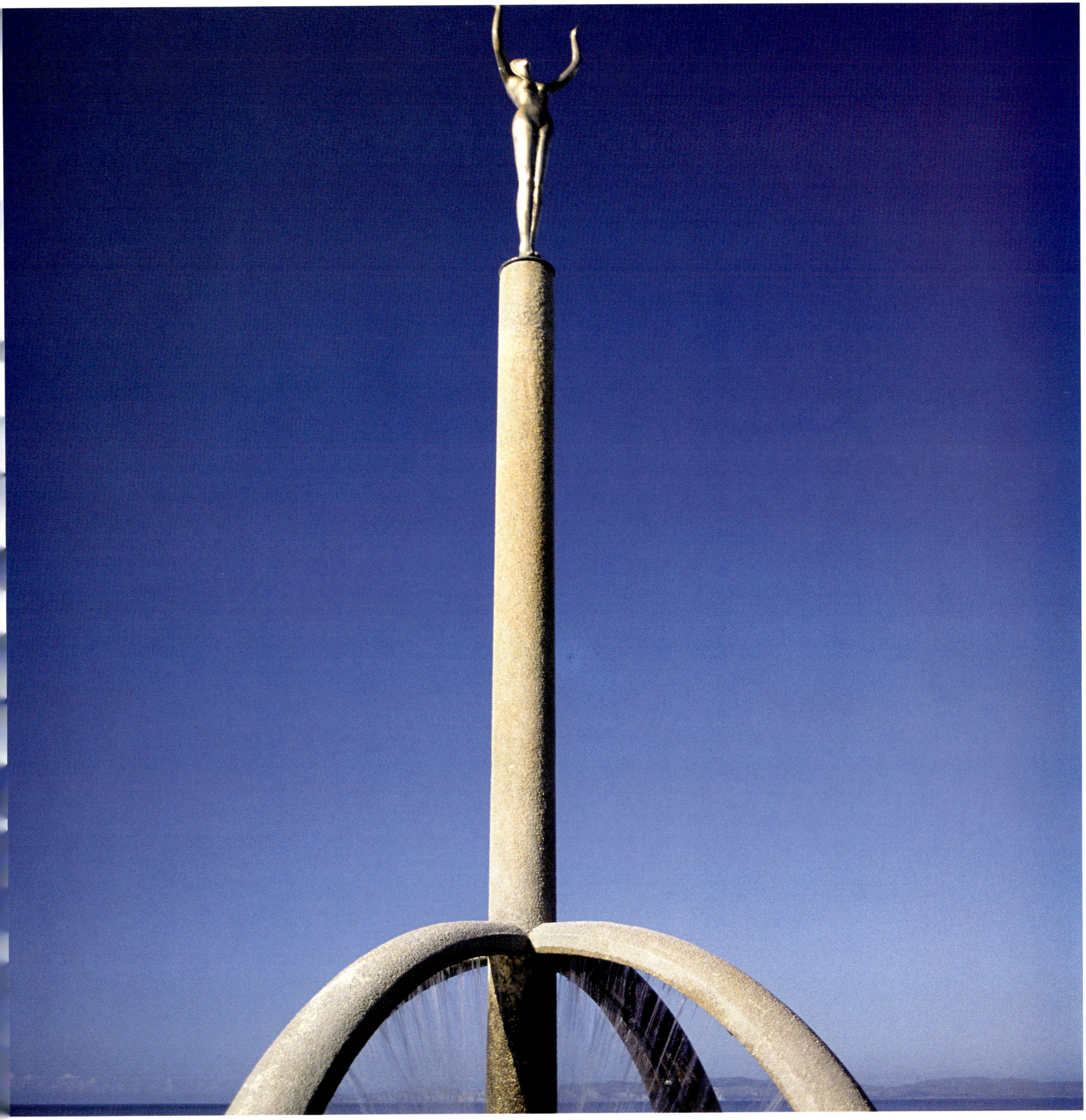

Vegetable Slice

Serves 4

Ingredients

flour for dusting
400 g store-bought puff pastry
1 egg, beaten
4 eggs, fried
baby salad leaves

Vegetable Filling

4 tbsp vegetable oil
1 small red onion, halved and sliced
1 red capsicum, cut in large dice
1 yellow capsicum, cut in large dice
2 small courgettes, sliced
8 fresh asparagus spears, cut in 3
2 cloves garlic, finely chopped
125 ml (½ cup) store-bought mayonnaise
salt and pepper

Preheat oven to 180°C.

Lightly dust work surface with flour. Roll pastry into a rectangle 34 cm long by 15 cm wide. Cut a 2-cm strip of pastry off each edge and set aside. Brush the pastry rectangle with egg. Place the strips of pastry around the edges of the rectangle and also brush with egg. Refrigerate for 30 minutes.

Before baking, prick pastry inside the edges with a fork. Fill with scrunched foil. Bake for 20–25 minutes or until golden brown.

Remove from oven and allow pastry to rest for 5 minutes. Remove foil. Scrape out the top layer of pastry inside the edges, so all that remains is the pastry shell. Meanwhile, make the Vegetable Filling.

To make the Vegetable Filling

Heat 2 tbsp oil in a large frying pan to a high heat. Add onion and capsicums. Cook for approximately 4 minutes, or until coloured and soft. Place in a colander to drain.

Wipe frying pan clean. Heat 2 tbsp oil to a high heat. Cook courgettes, asparagus and garlic for approximately 3 minutes, or until soft. Add to the colander.

Place half the drained vegetables in a bowl. Mix in mayonnaise. Season with salt and pepper to taste.

Assembly

Spread the Vegetable Filling with mayonnaise in pastry case. Top with remaining Vegetable Filling. Reheat in oven for 5 minutes and then slice into 4. Fry the eggs then serve each slice topped with an egg and a few baby salad leaves.

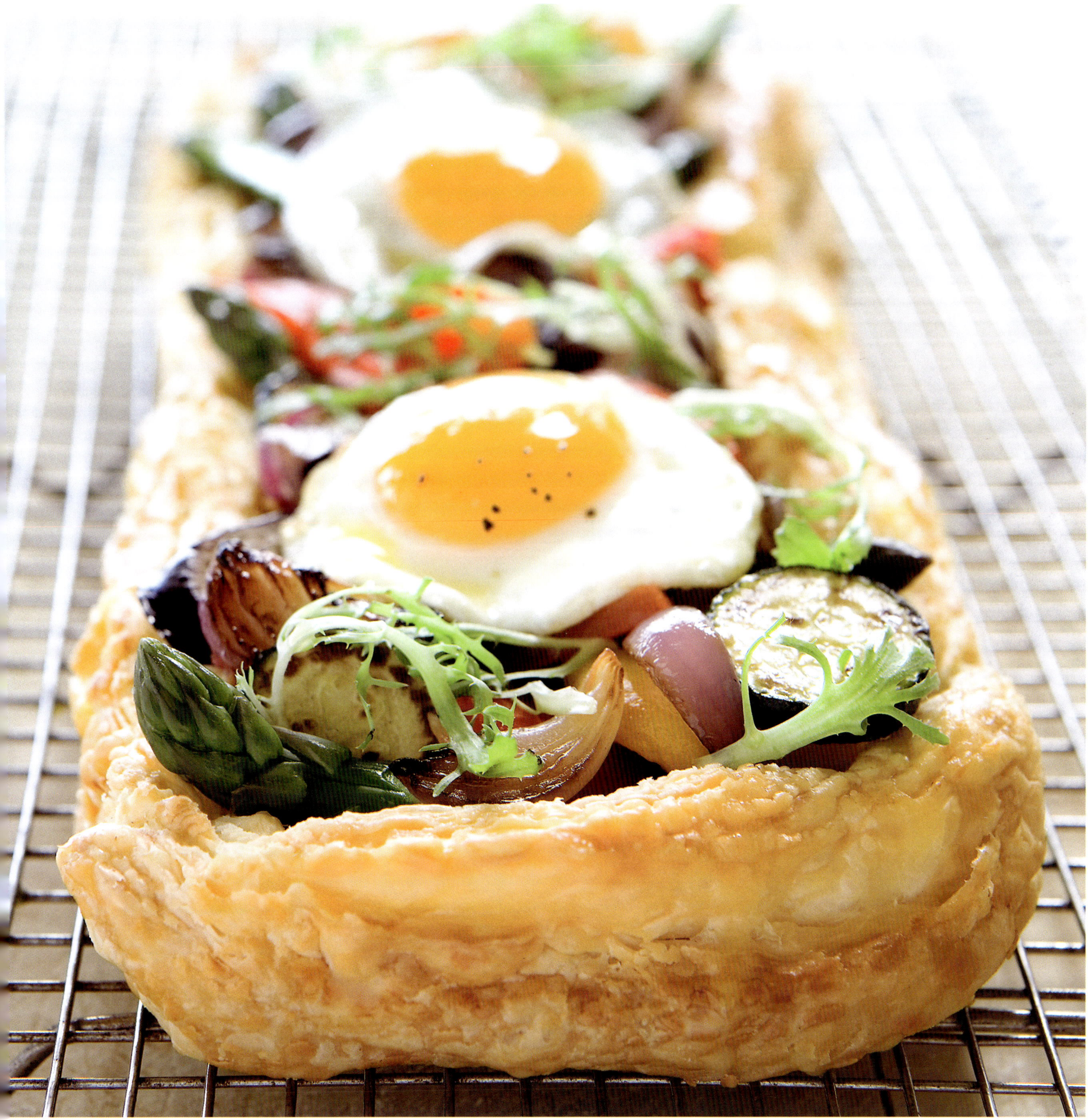

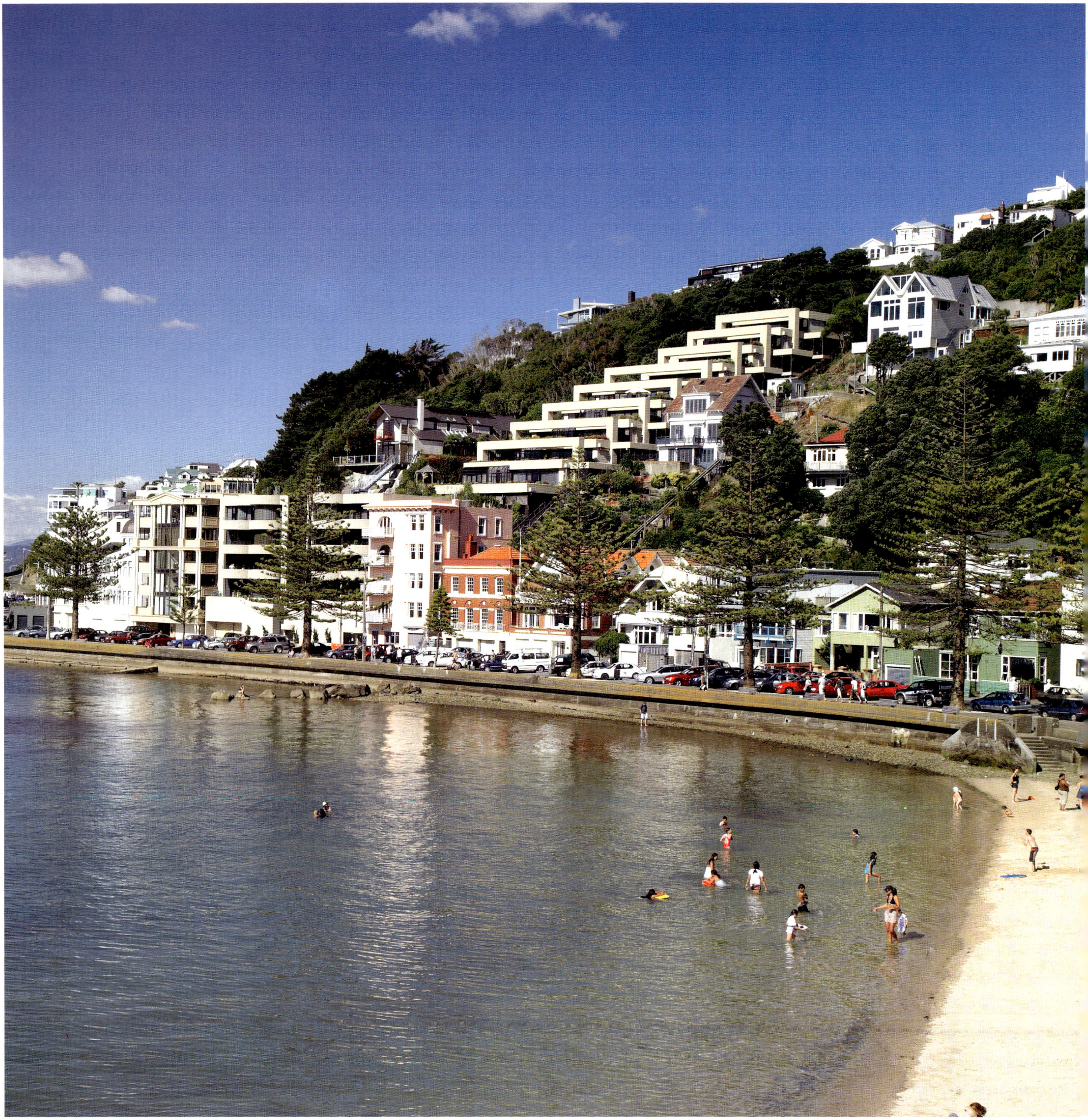

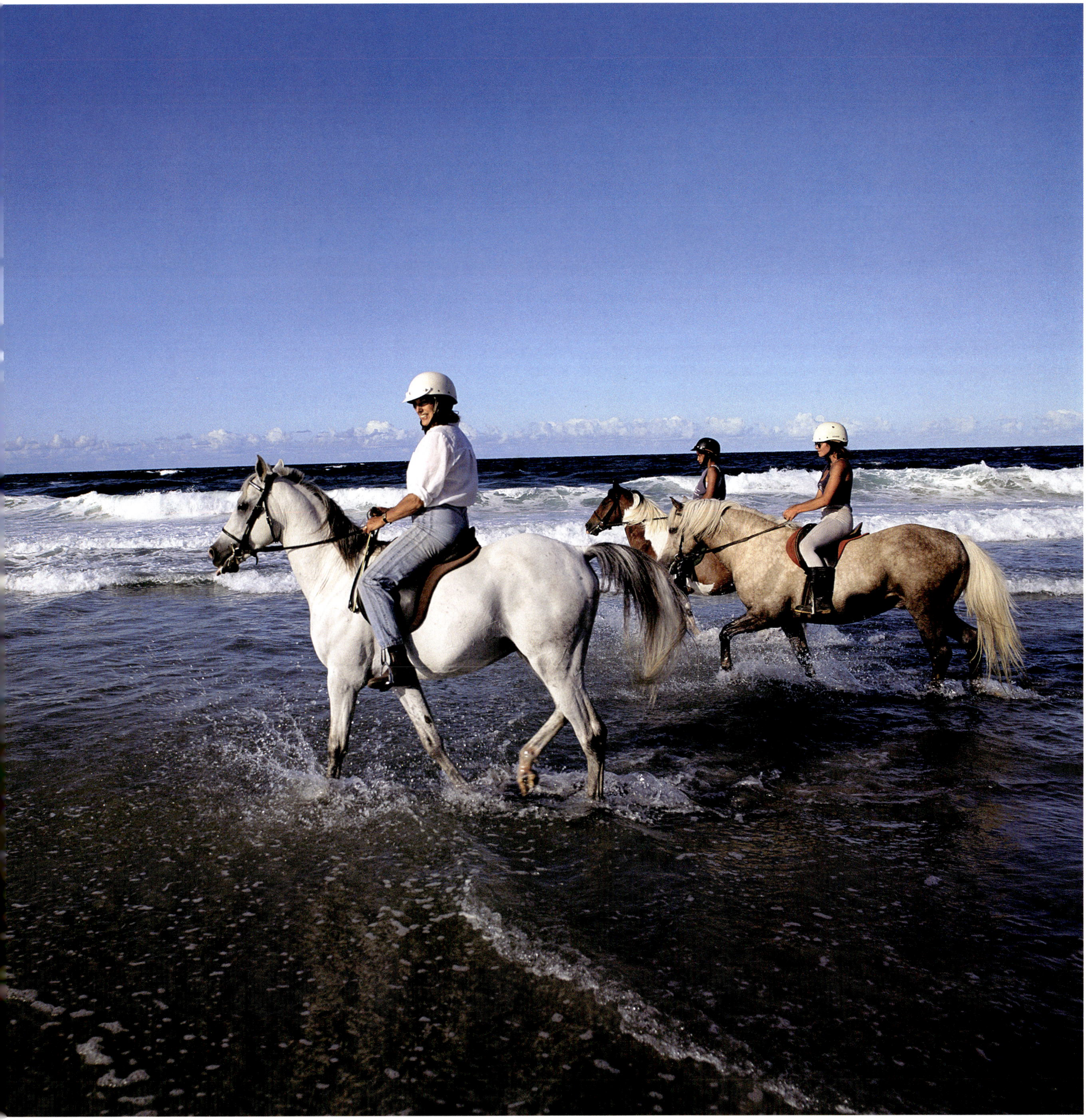

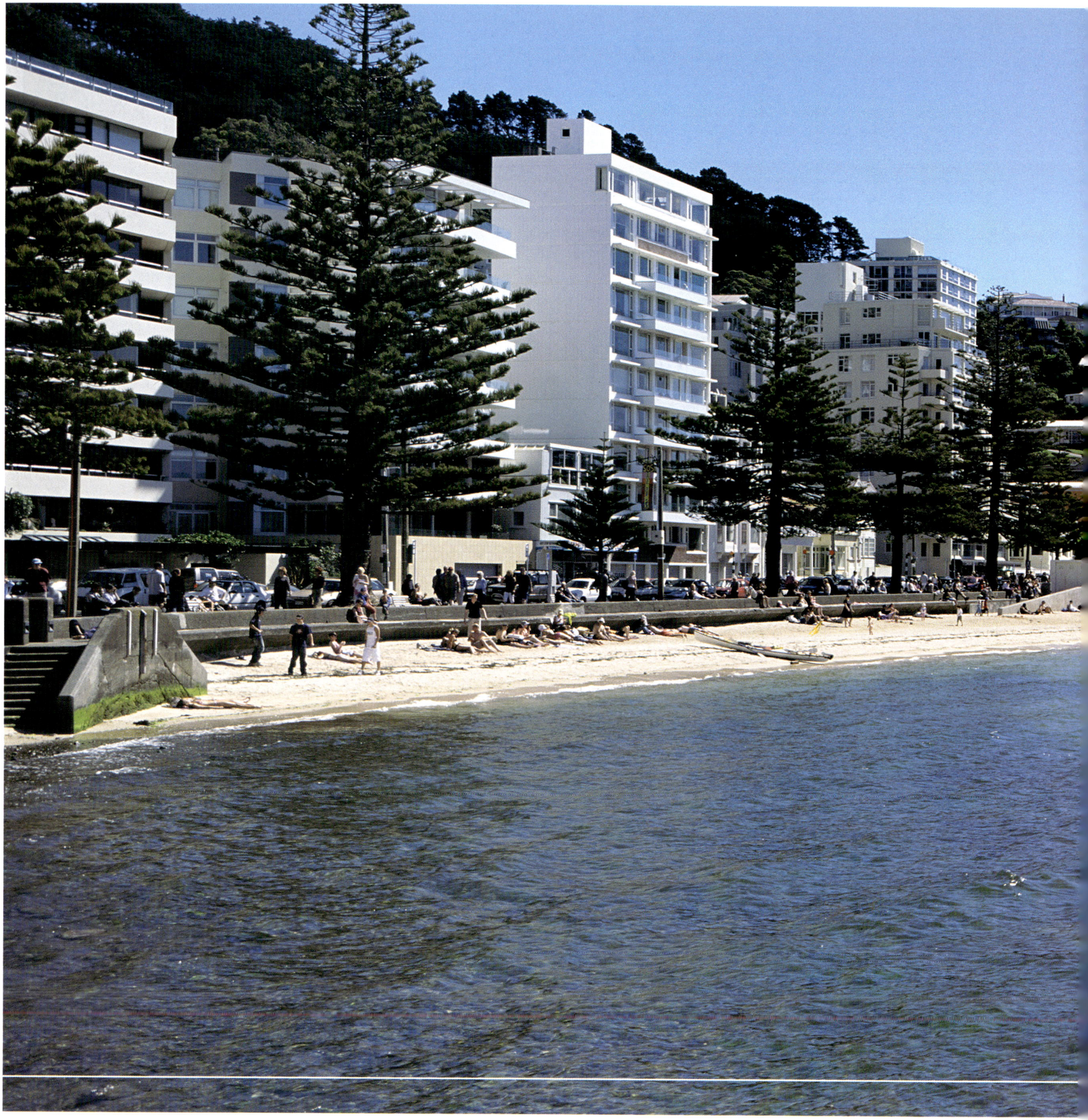

Light Mains

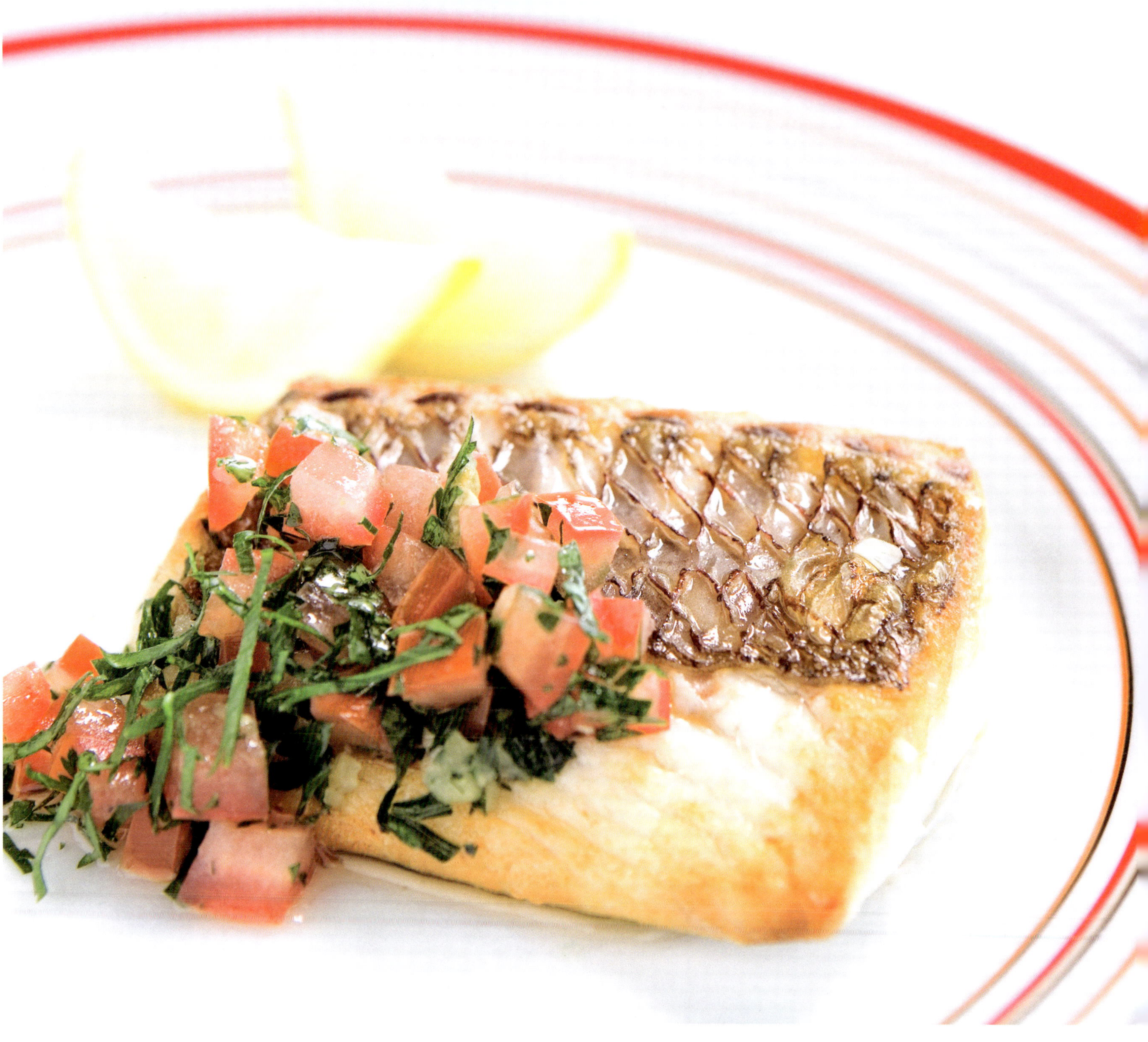

Crispy Skinned Snapper with Tomato and Parsley Salad

Serves 4

Ingredients

4 x 180 g snapper fillets, skin on
flour for dusting
salt and pepper
3 tbsp canola oil

Tomato and Parsley Salad
3 medium tomatoes
1 clove garlic, finely chopped
2 tbsp shredded flat-leaf parsley
2 tbsp canola oil
salt and pepper

Lemon Butter
200 g butter
juice of 1 lemon

Make the Tomato and Parsley Salad and set aside. Dust both sides of the snapper with flour. Sprinkle with salt and pepper.

Heat oil in a large frying pan to a medium to hot heat. Cook the snapper, skin side down. When golden and crispy, turn the pieces of fish over and lower the heat.

Cook for approximately 4 minutes, depending on thickness of fish. Remove from pan to serving plates and keep warm. Set pan aside and make the Lemon Butter.

To make the Tomato and Parsley Salad
Deseed the tomatoes and cut into a medium dice. Place them in a bowl with garlic, parsley and oil. Mix well. Season with salt and pepper to taste.

To make the Lemon Butter
Put butter and lemon juice in the frying pan the fish was cooked in. Heat until hot, but do not allow to boil.

Assembly

Divide the Tomato and Parsley Salad between plates. Place 1 piece of fish on each plate and spoon Lemon Butter over fish. Serve with fries and salad.

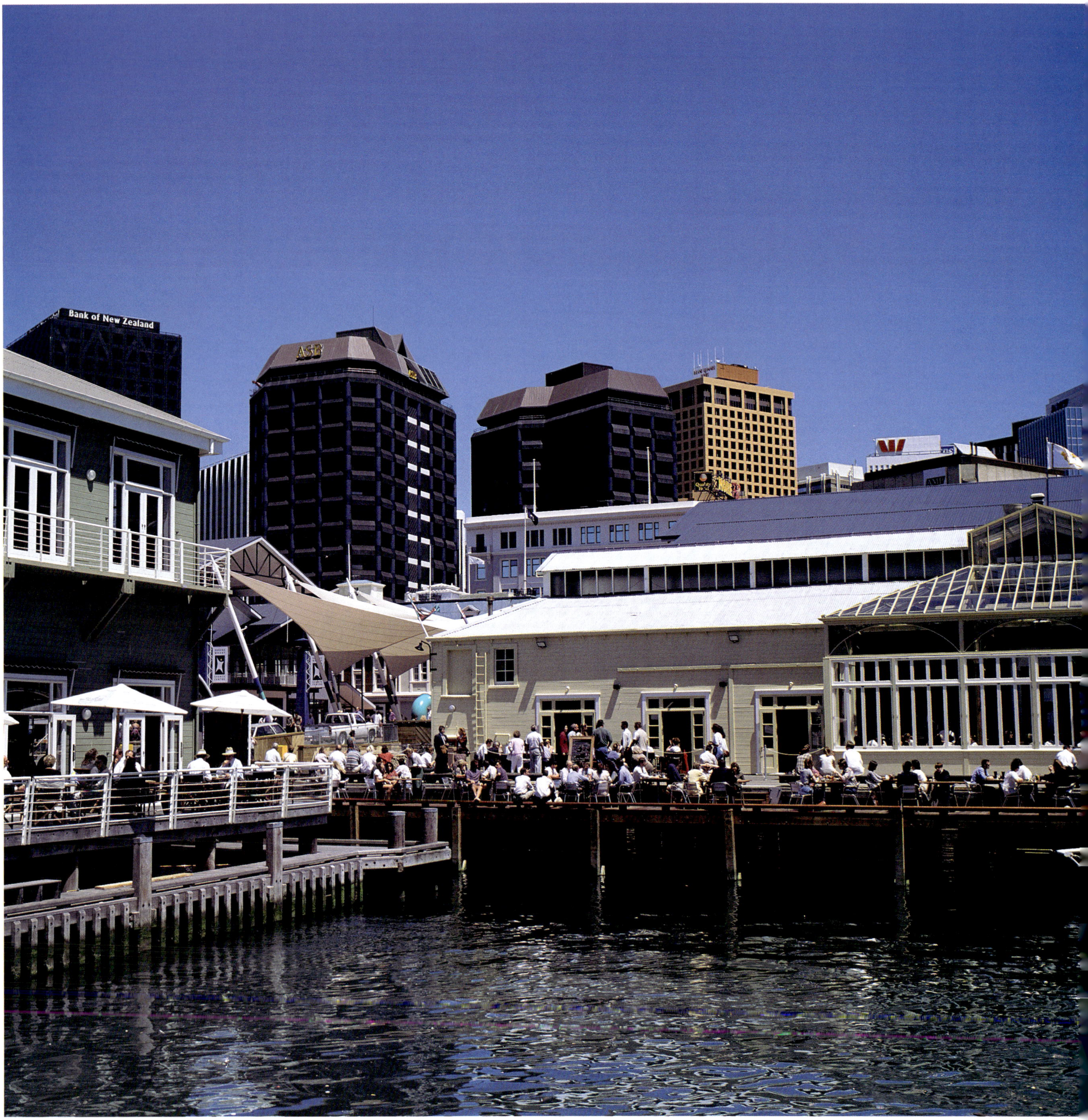
Bank of New Zealand
ASB

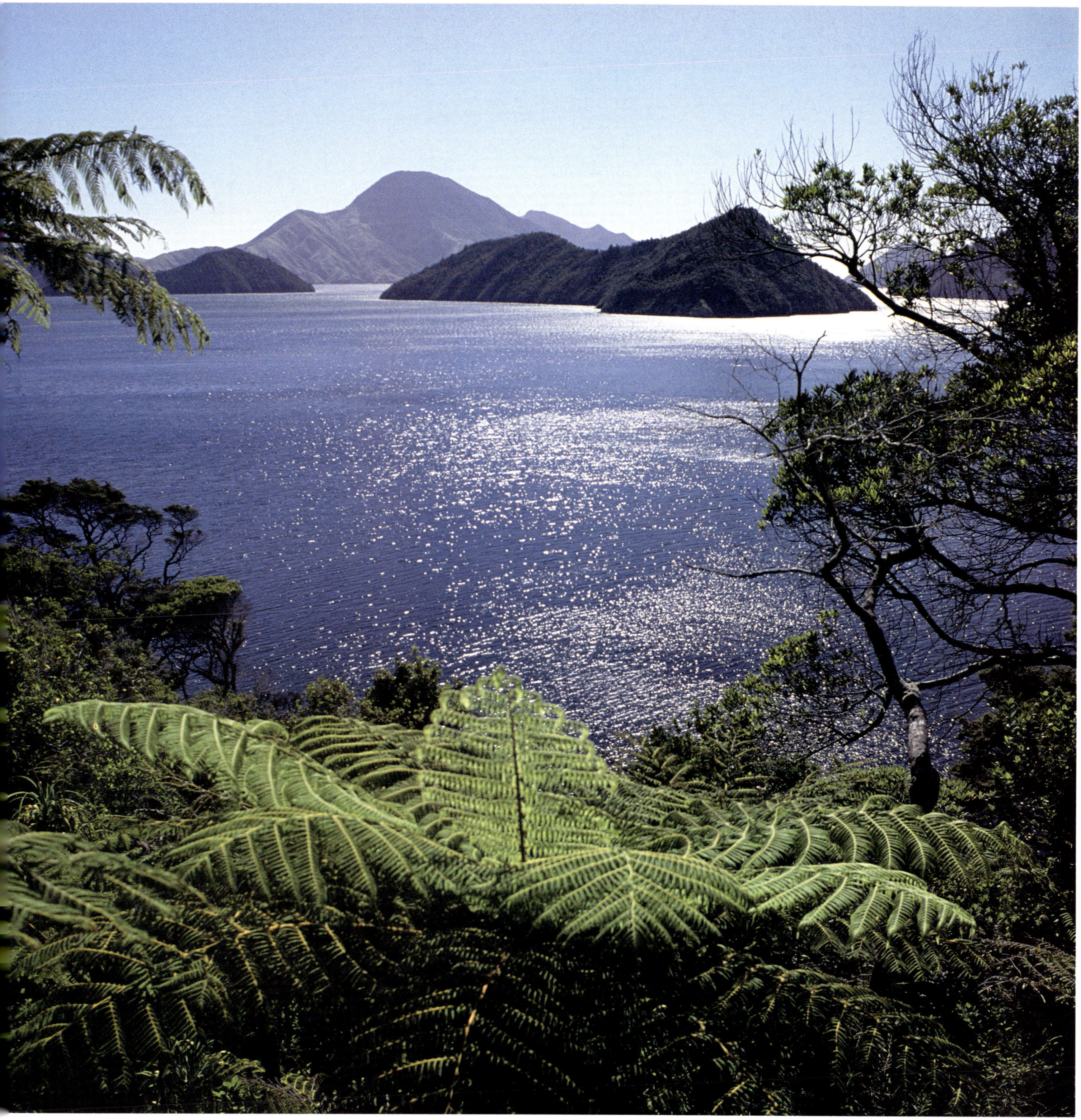

Fish Cakes and Prawns with an Avocado Oil and Caper Dressing

Serves 6

Ingredients

500 g raw fish, either Hoki, Gurnard,
 Snapper or Salmon
½ cup diced onion
½ cup diced celery
½ cup grated carrot
¼ cup chopped parsley
1 large egg
½ cup breadcrumbs
extra breadcrumbs for coating
salt and pepper
2 tbsp canola oil
18 uncooked prawn cutlets
baby salad leaves

Avocado Oil and Caper Dressing

60 ml (¼ cup) avocado oil
3 tbsp capers
1 tsp sugar
zest and juice of 1 lime
salt and pepper

Make the Avocado Oil and Caper Dressing and set aside.
Preheat oven to 180°C.
Mix together fish, onion, celery, carrot, parsley, egg and breadcrumbs. Season with salt and pepper to taste.
Form mixture into 6 fish cakes. Coat each fish cake well with remaining breadcrumbs.
Heat oil in a frying pan to a moderate heat. Cook the fish cakes for approximately 3 minutes on each side until golden brown.
Place on a tray in oven. Turn oven off.
In the same pan, fry the prawns for 1 minute on each side. Sprinkle with salt and pepper.

To make the Avocado Oil and Caper Dressing

In a bowl, mix together avocado oil, capers, sugar and lime zest and juice. Season with salt and pepper to taste.

Assembly

Place 1 fish cake, 3 prawns and a few baby salad leaves on each plate. Drizzle with Avocado Oil and Caper Dressing and serve.

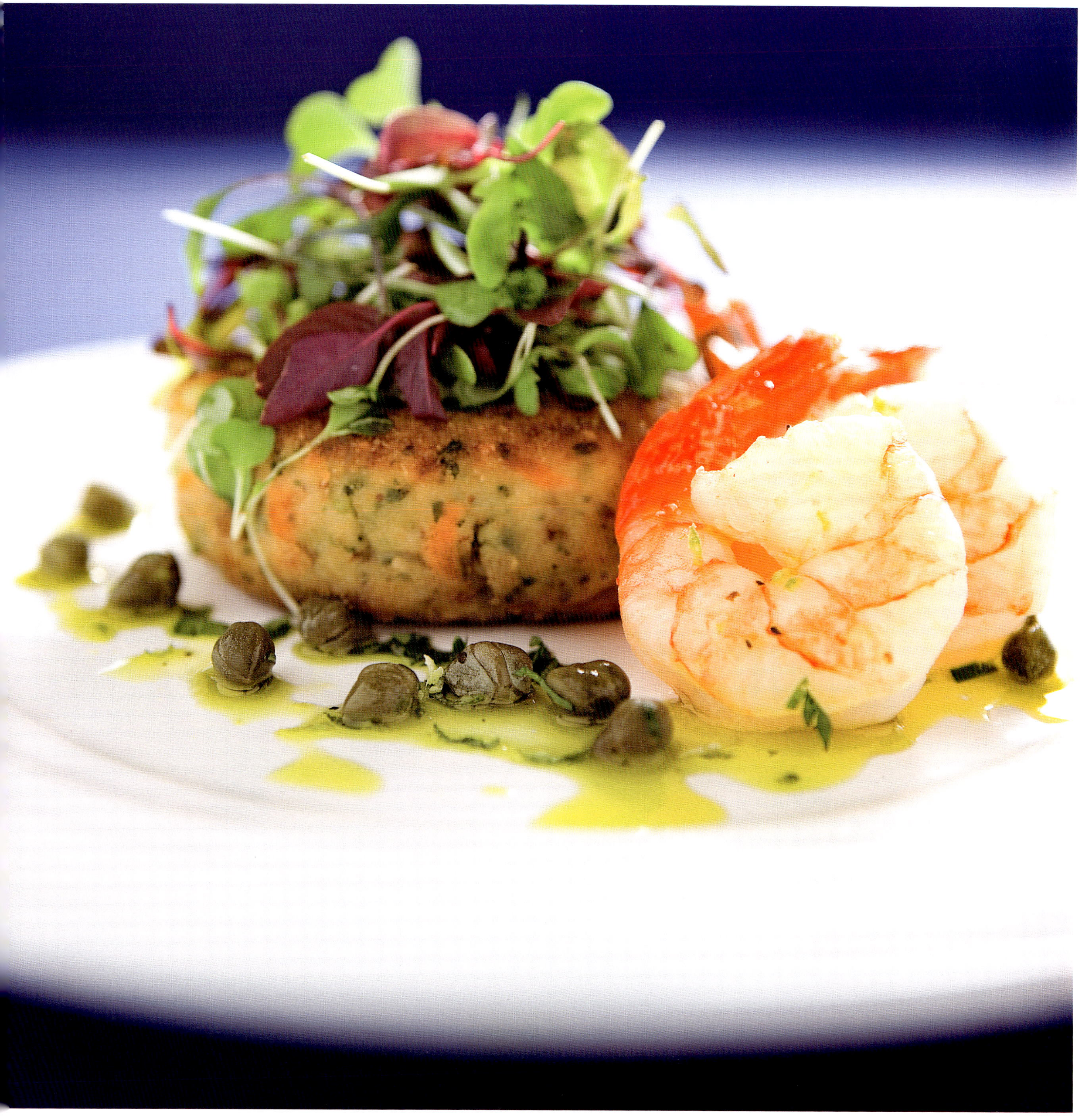

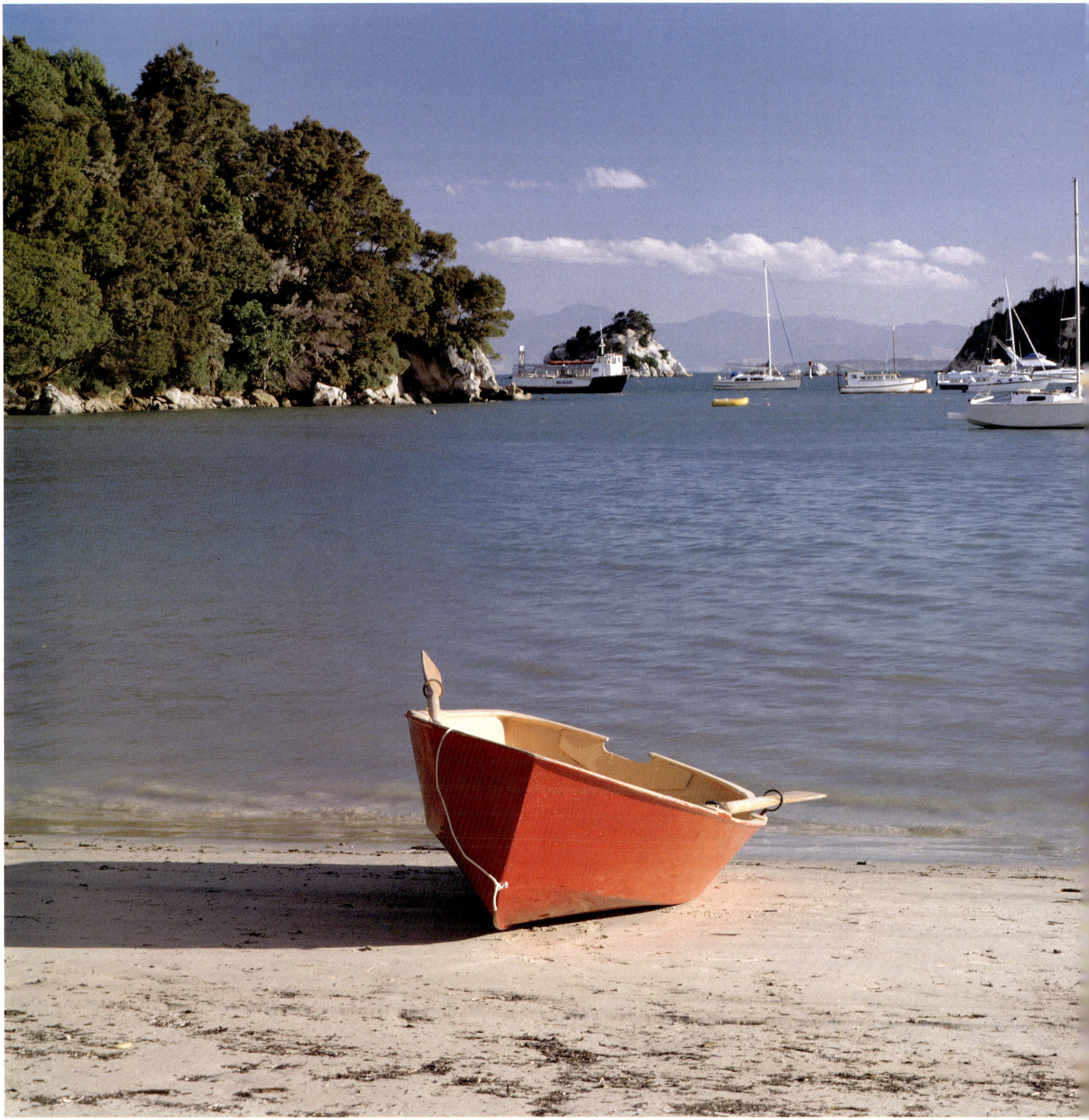

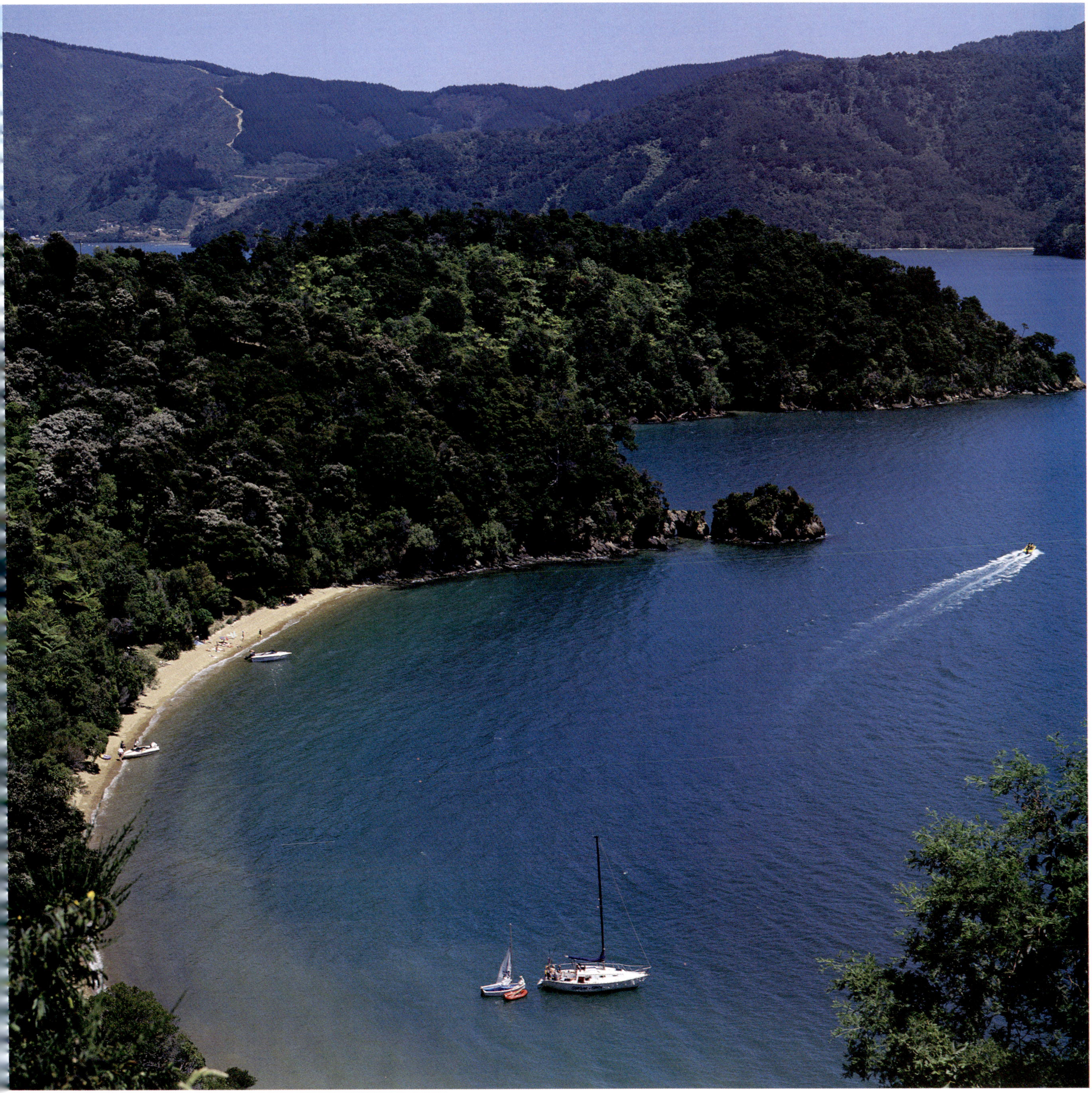

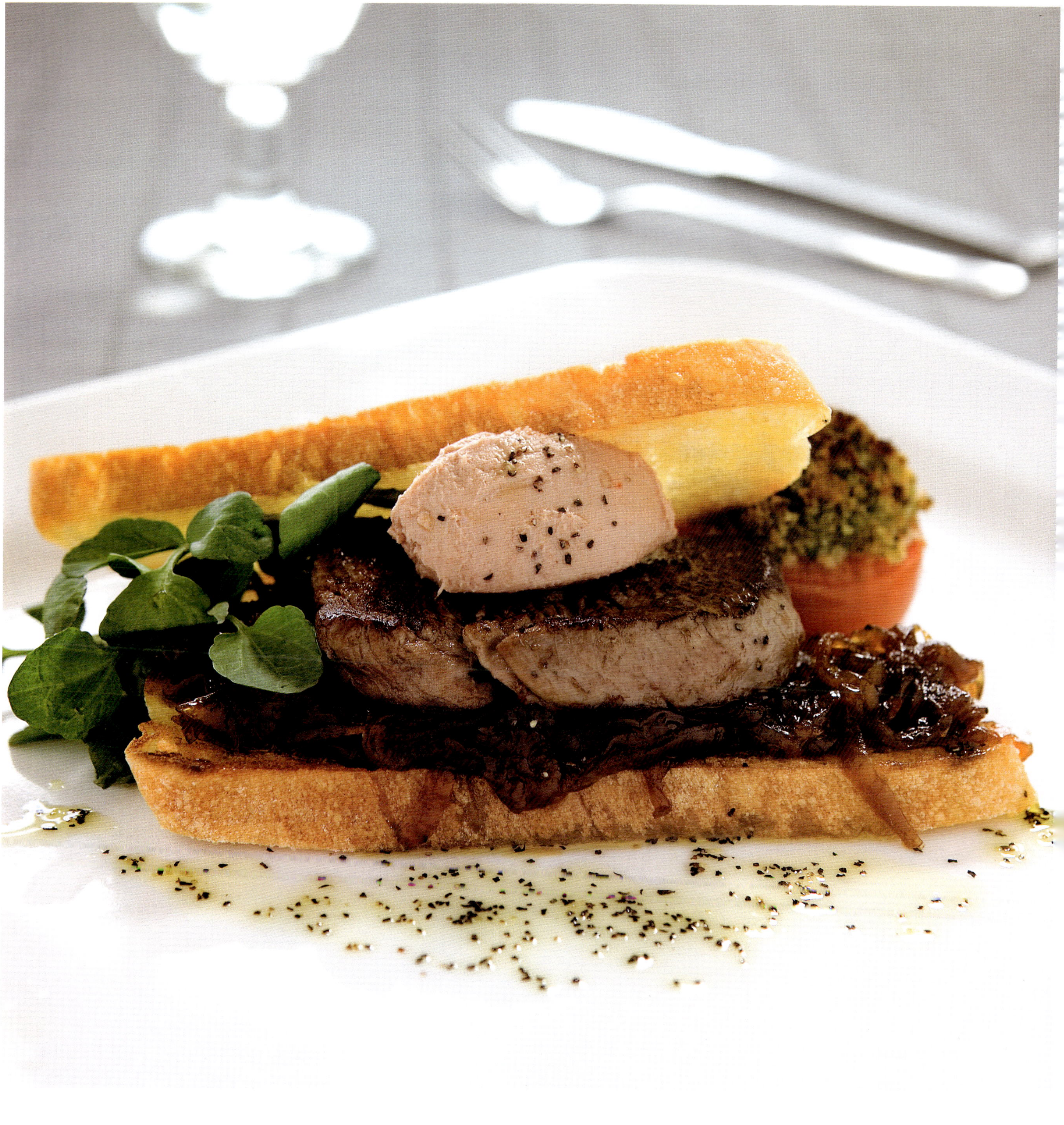

Gourmet Steak Sandwich

Serves 4

Ingredients

4 x 90 g 2-cm-thick beef fillet steaks
salt and pepper
200 g soft butter
8 slices good quality bread
3 tbsp canola oil
1 tbsp fine cracked pepper
salt to taste
125 ml (½ cup) store-bought onion jam
250 ml (1 cup) watercress leaves
4 tbsp chicken and Cognac pâté

Preheat oven to 125°C.
Sprinkle each side of the steaks with salt and pepper. Heat 2 tbsp butter in a large frying pan. When the butter starts to brown add the steaks. Cook 2 steaks at a time, for 1 minute on each side. Place steaks on a tray in the warm oven.
Butter the bread on both sides. Place on a tray and lightly toast each side under the grill in your oven.
In a bowl, mix together canola oil and cracked pepper. Add a little salt to taste.

Assembly

Place 1 slice of bread on each plate. Spread with onion jam, then place watercress leaves on top. Place a steak on top of watercress and top with 1 tbsp pâté. Drizzle the sandwich with black pepper oil. Top with another slice of bread and serve.

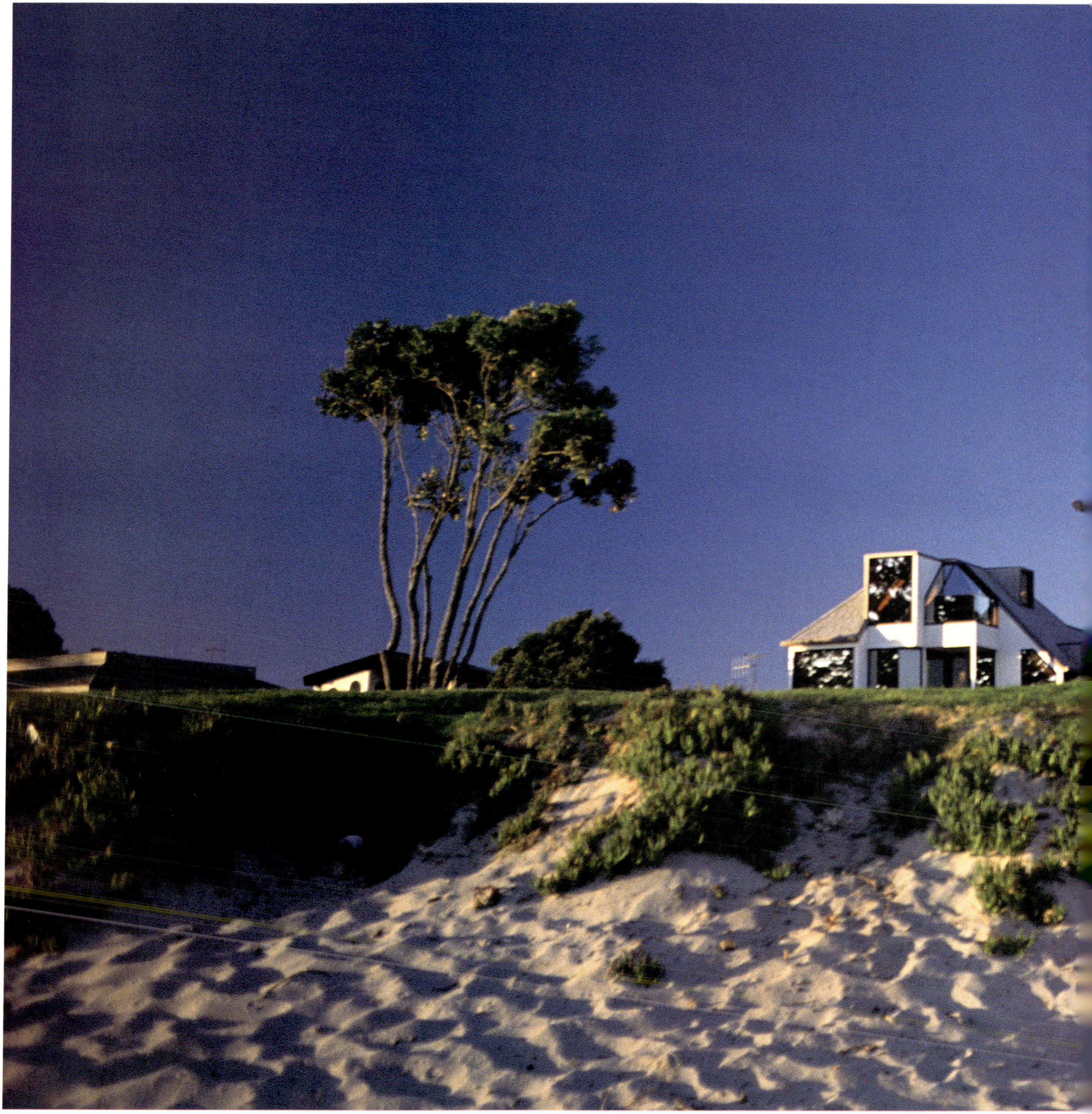

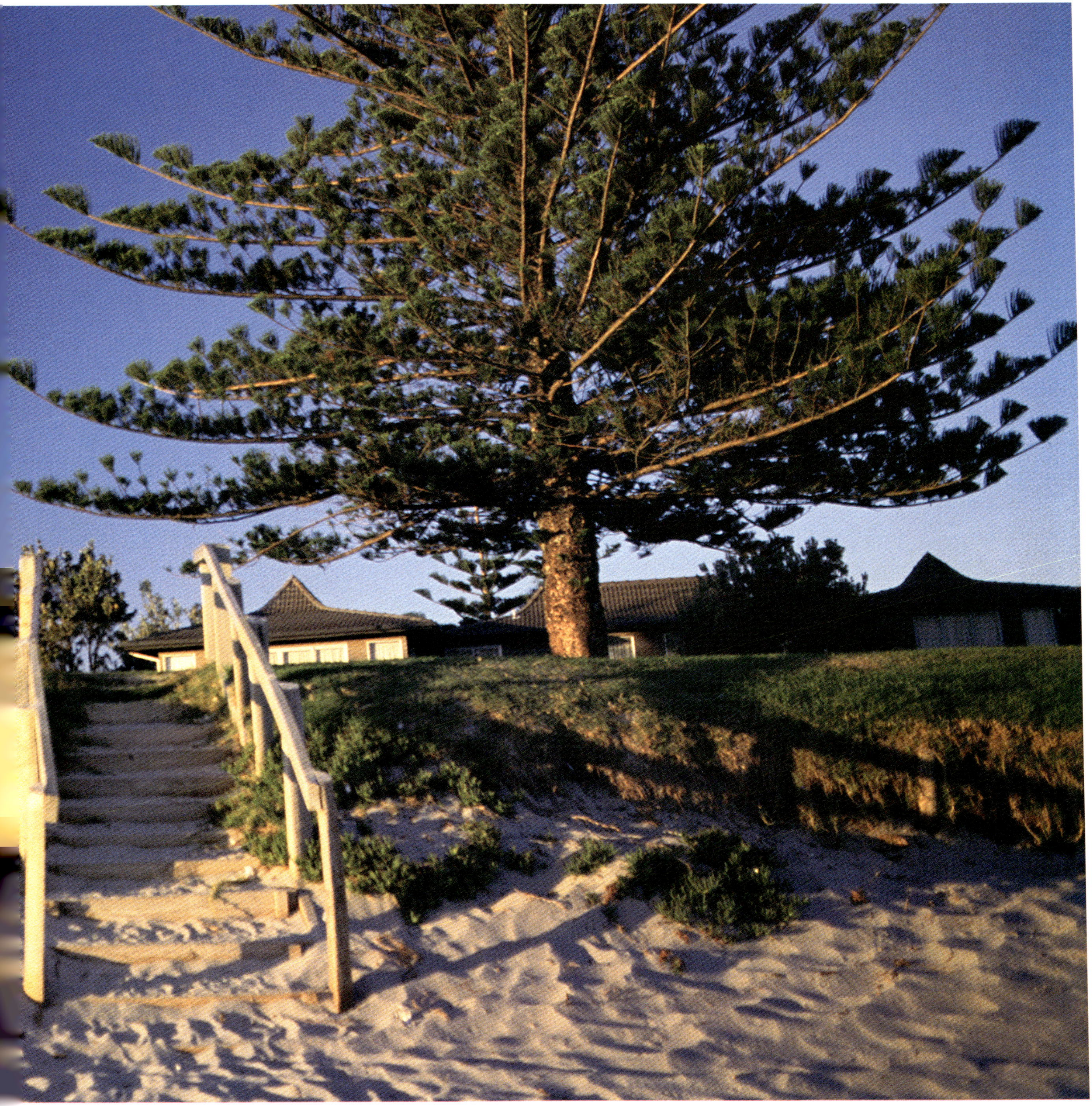

Honeyed Pork, Goat Cheese and Apple Salad with Citrus Dressing

Serves 4

Ingredients

1 trimmed pork fillet (approximately 350 g)
60 ml (¼ cup) clear honey
2 tbsp canola oil
salt and pepper
1 green apple, skin on
1 red apple, skin on
120 g goat cheese, sliced
2 cups watercress leaves

Citrus Dressing

1 tsp each of lemon, orange and lime zest
1 tsp each of lemon, orange and lime juice
2 tsp sugar
60 ml (¼ cup) canola oil
salt and pepper

Make the Citrus Dressing and set aside.
Cut pork into 3 pieces. Place in a bowl with honey. Coat well. Refrigerate for 30 minutes, turning occasionally.
Preheat oven to 200°C.
Heat oil in a frying pan to a medium heat. Add the pork. Cook until golden brown and well-sealed, approximately 2 minutes each side.
Place on an oven tray. Sprinkle with salt and pepper. Cook in oven for 10 minutes.
Remove from oven. Rest for 5 minutes, slice into 12–16 pieces.
Cut apples into quarters, core and slice.
In a salad bowl, gently toss apple, goat cheese and watercress with ⅔ Citrus Dressing.

To make the Citrus Dressing

Place zest, juice, sugar and oil in a jar with a tight-fitting lid. Shake well. Season with salt and pepper to taste.

Assembly

Build a small tower of salad and pork on each plate, reserving 2 slices of pork for top. Drizzle with remaining Citrus Dressing and serve.

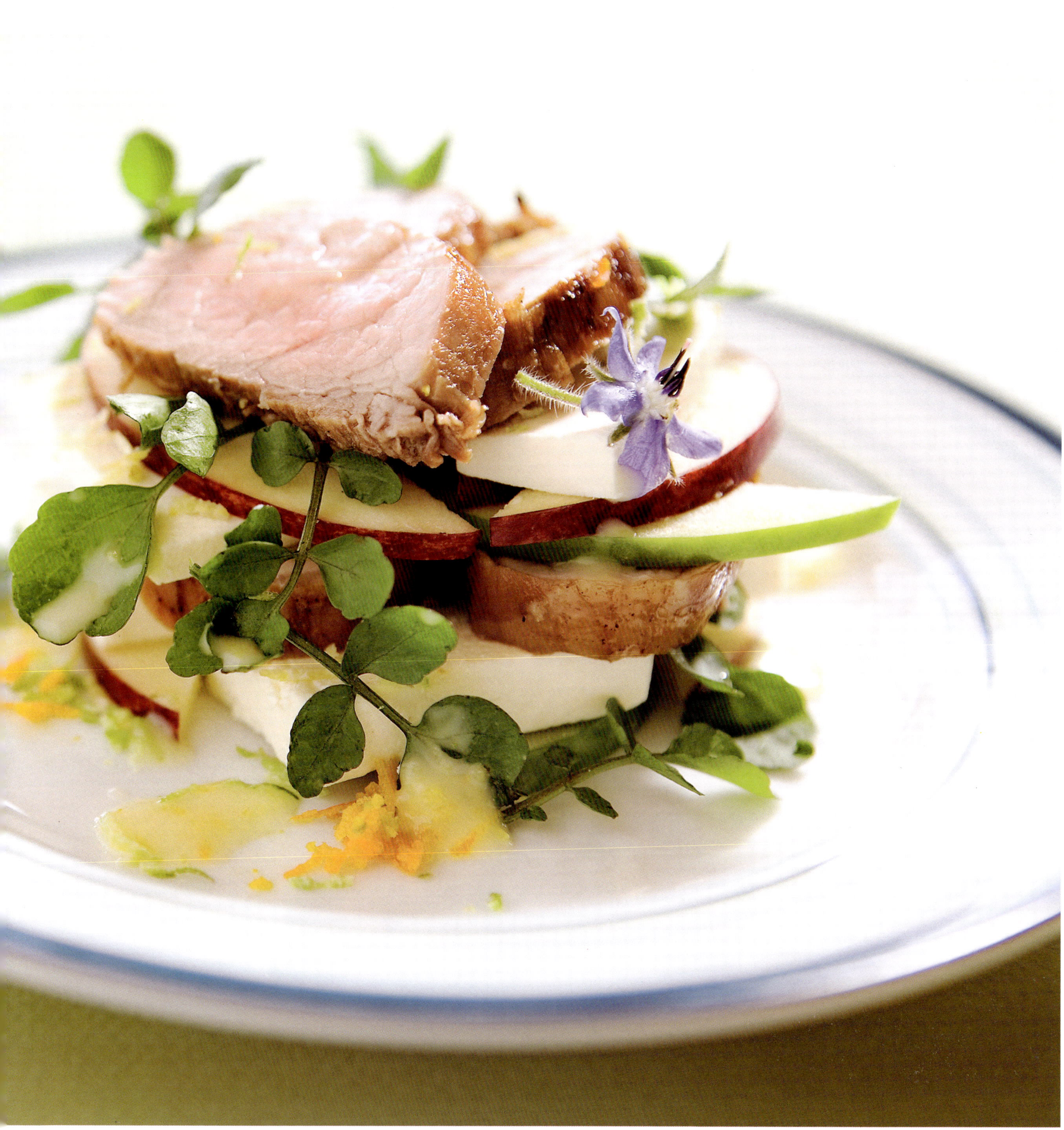

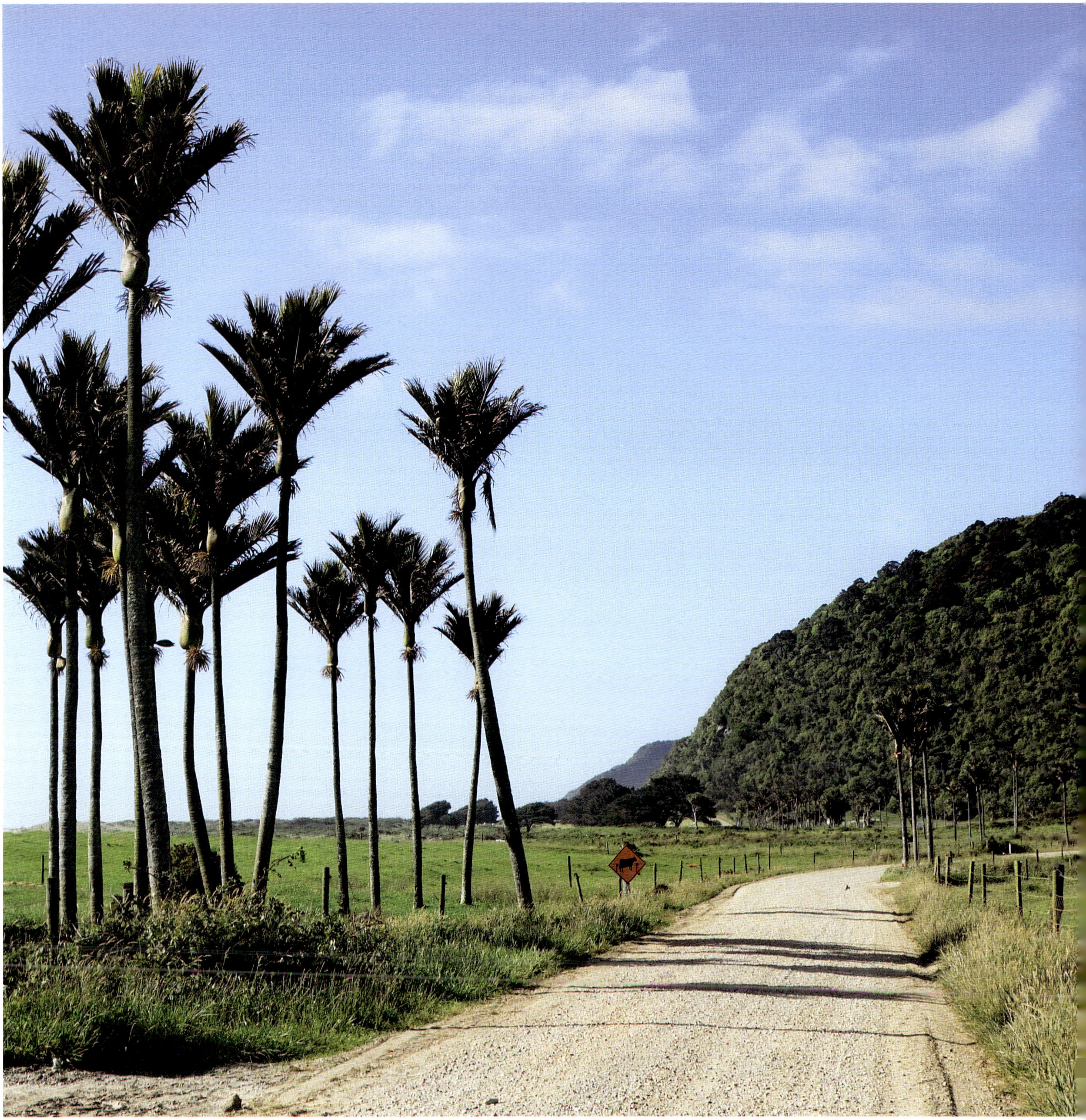

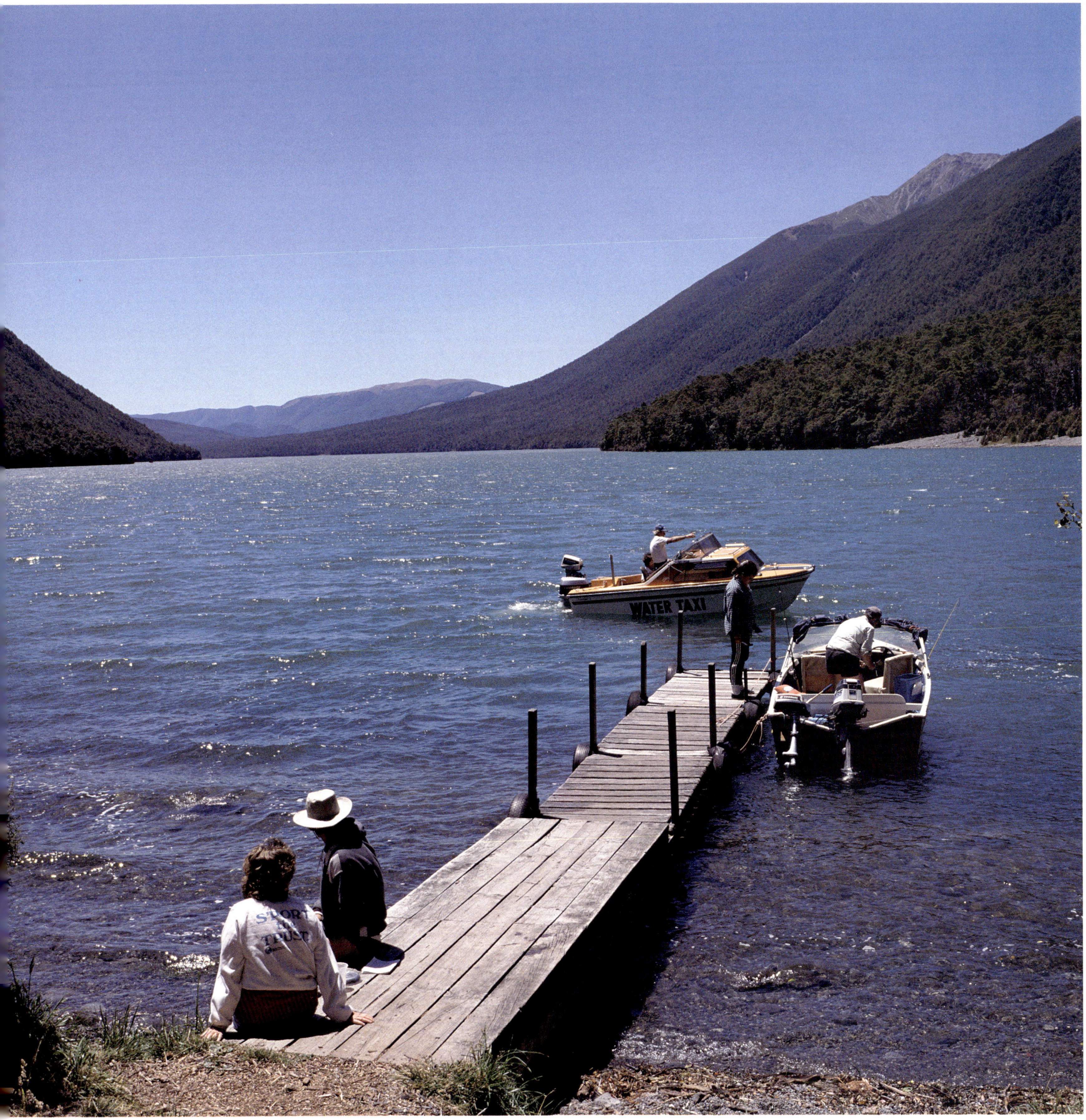
WATER TAXI

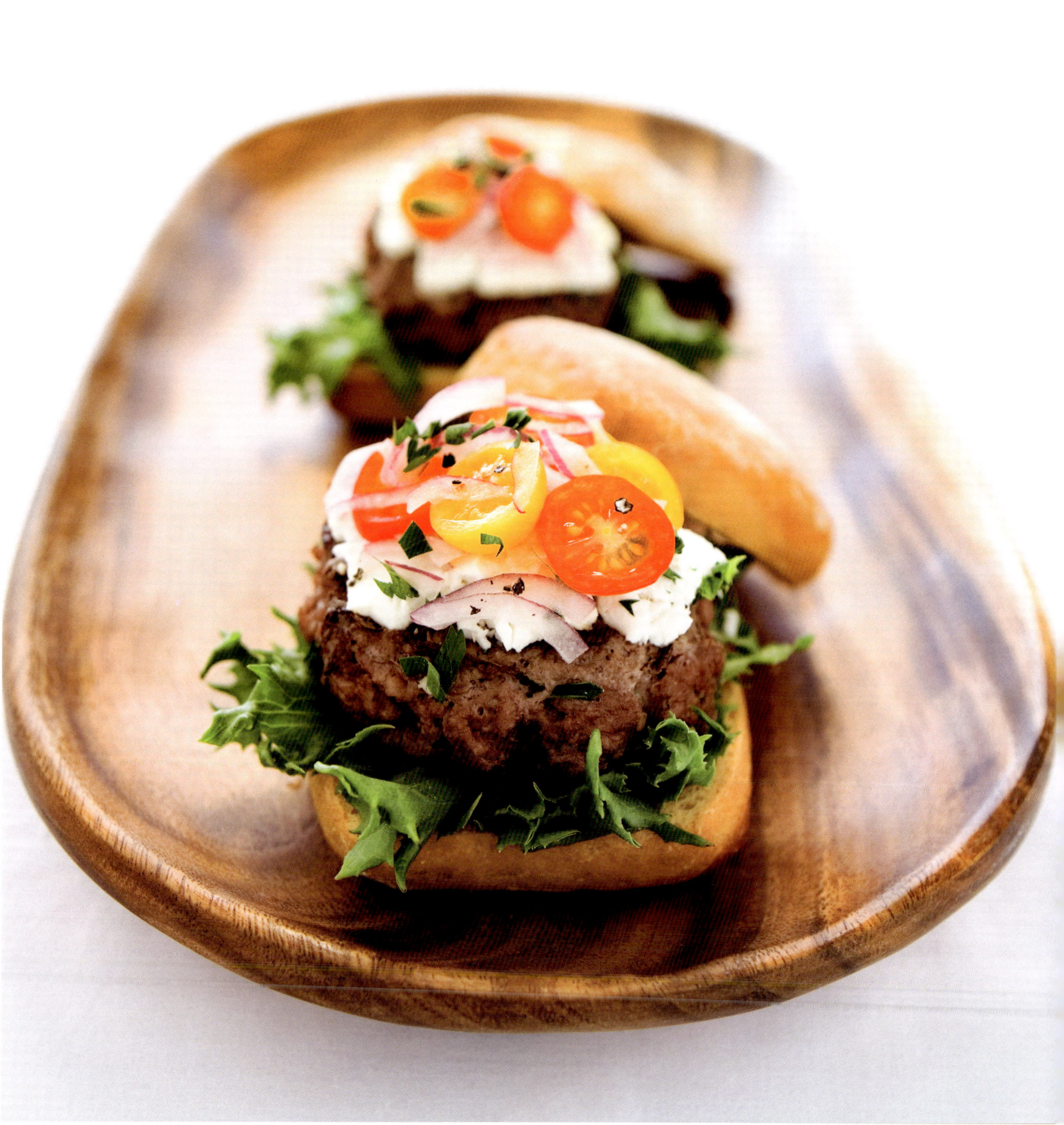

Minted Lamb Burgers with Feta

Serves 4

Ingredients

500 g lamb mince
2 cloves garlic, finely chopped
3 tbsp finely chopped mint
salt and pepper
2 tbsp canola oil
4 x 40-g slices feta cheese
4 quality burger buns or rolls
soft butter
125 ml (½ cup) store-bought
  mayonnaise
salad leaves
8 cherry tomatoes, sliced
½ small red onion, thinly sliced
2 tbsp chopped parsley

Combine mince, garlic and mint in a bowl. Season with salt and pepper to taste.

Form the mixture into 4 patties. Cover and refrigerate.

Heat canola oil in a frying pan to a medium heat. If using a barbecue, brush the grill with oil.

Cook patties for 5 minutes on one side. Turn, then place 1 slice feta cheese on each burger. Cook for another 5 minutes or to your liking.

Spread buns with butter. Toast buns, cut side up, under grill. If using a barbecue, brush buns with oil and cook until golden brown.

Assembly

Spread mayonnaise on all toasted buns. Cover the bun bases with salad leaves. Place 1 pattie on bun, feta side up. Top with sliced tomato, red onion and parsley. Serve with kumara chips, wedges or fries.

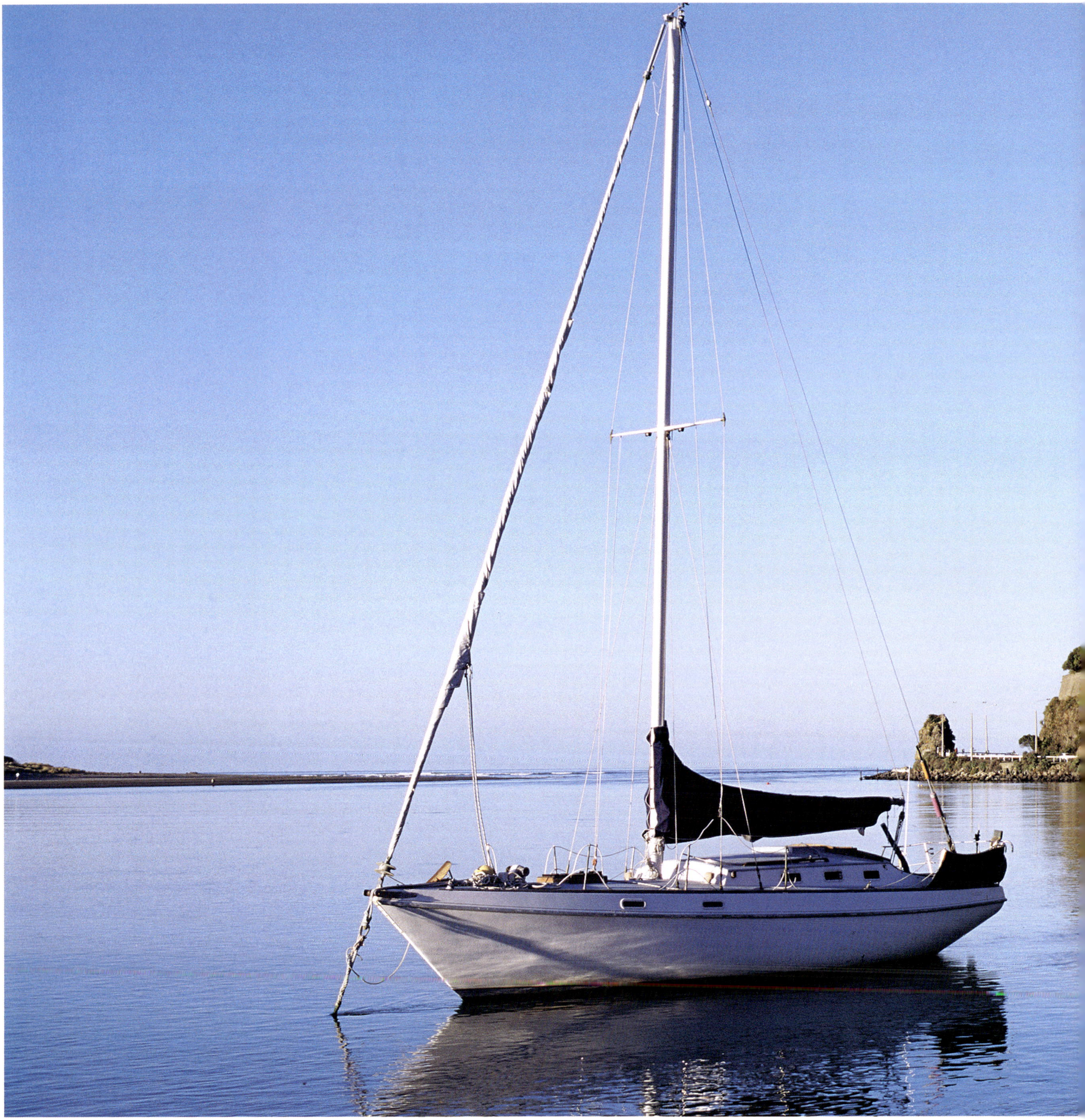

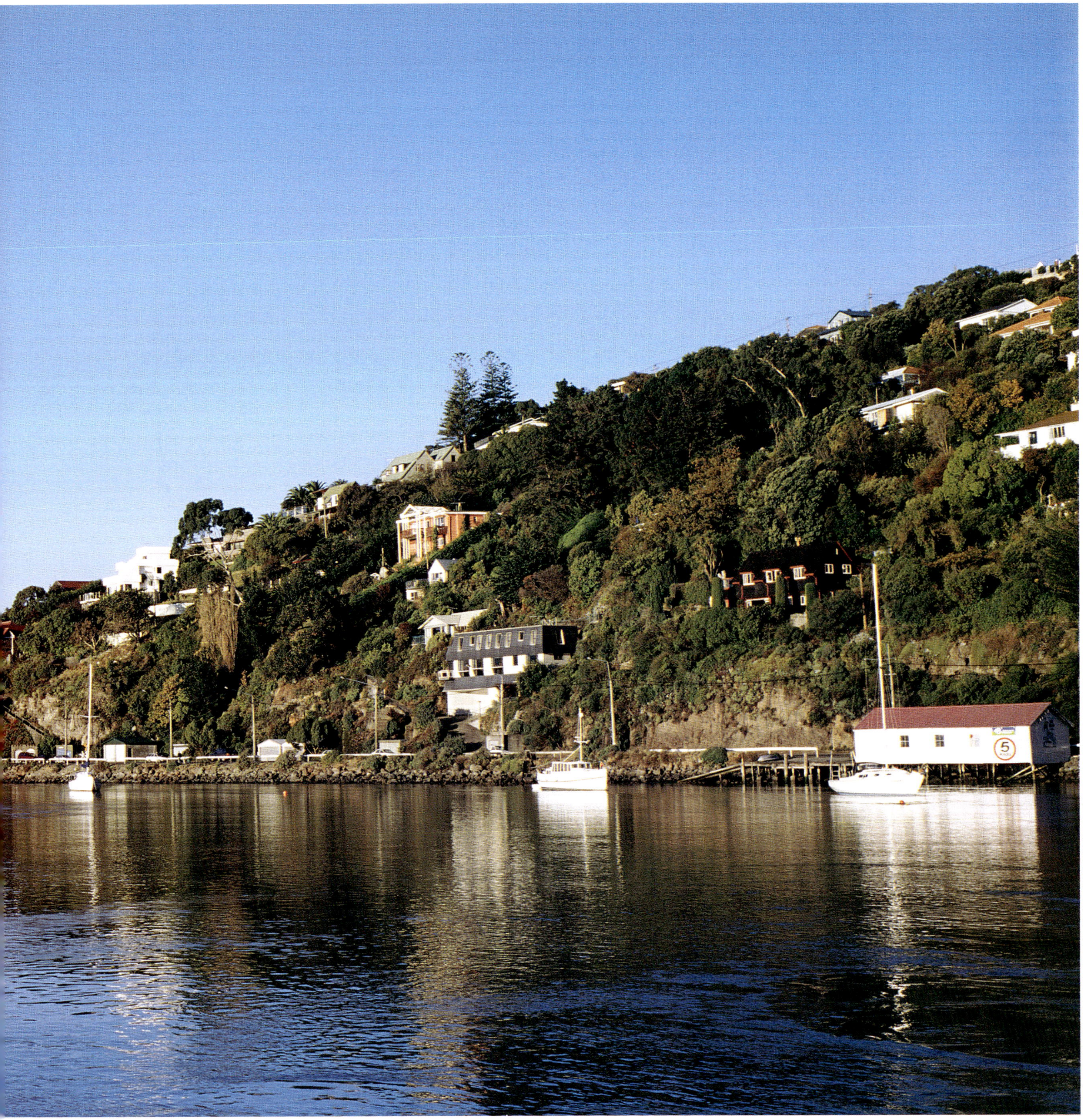

Mussels with a Parsley Crust and Tomato Salad

Serves 4

Ingredients

20 fresh mussels
500 ml (2 cups) water
1 tsp salt
a few parsley stalks
2 cloves garlic, flattened
100 g melted butter
1½ cups coarse breadcrumbs
½ cup chopped parsley
salt and pepper
250 ml (1 cup) store-bought, thick mayonnaise
1 tsp finely chopped garlic

Tomato Salad

16 cherry tomatoes, halved
1 spring onion, finely sliced
2 tbsp chopped parsley
4 tbsp extra virgin olive oil or canola oil
salt and pepper

Preheat oven to 220°C.

Pull any hairy bits off the mussels and discard any open ones.

In a large, lidded saucepan, bring the water to the boil with the salt, parsley stalks and garlic. Add mussels. Replace lid and steam until all the mussels are open, discarding any that remain closed.

Once cool enough to handle, remove mussels from the shells, pull the hard pieces (the tongue) in the mussel out and place each mussel back in the half shell. Place the mussels on an oven tray.

In a bowl, mix together melted butter, breadcrumbs and parsley. Season with salt and pepper to taste. Top each mussel generously with the crust mixture. Bake until crust is golden brown.

In a separate bowl, mix together mayonnaise and garlic.

To make the Tomato Salad

Place tomatoes, spring onion, parsley and oil in a salad bowl. Mix together lightly. Season with salt and pepper to taste.

Assembly

Divide the Tomato Salad between 4 plates. Place 5 mussels and a dollop of mayonnaise on each plate and serve.

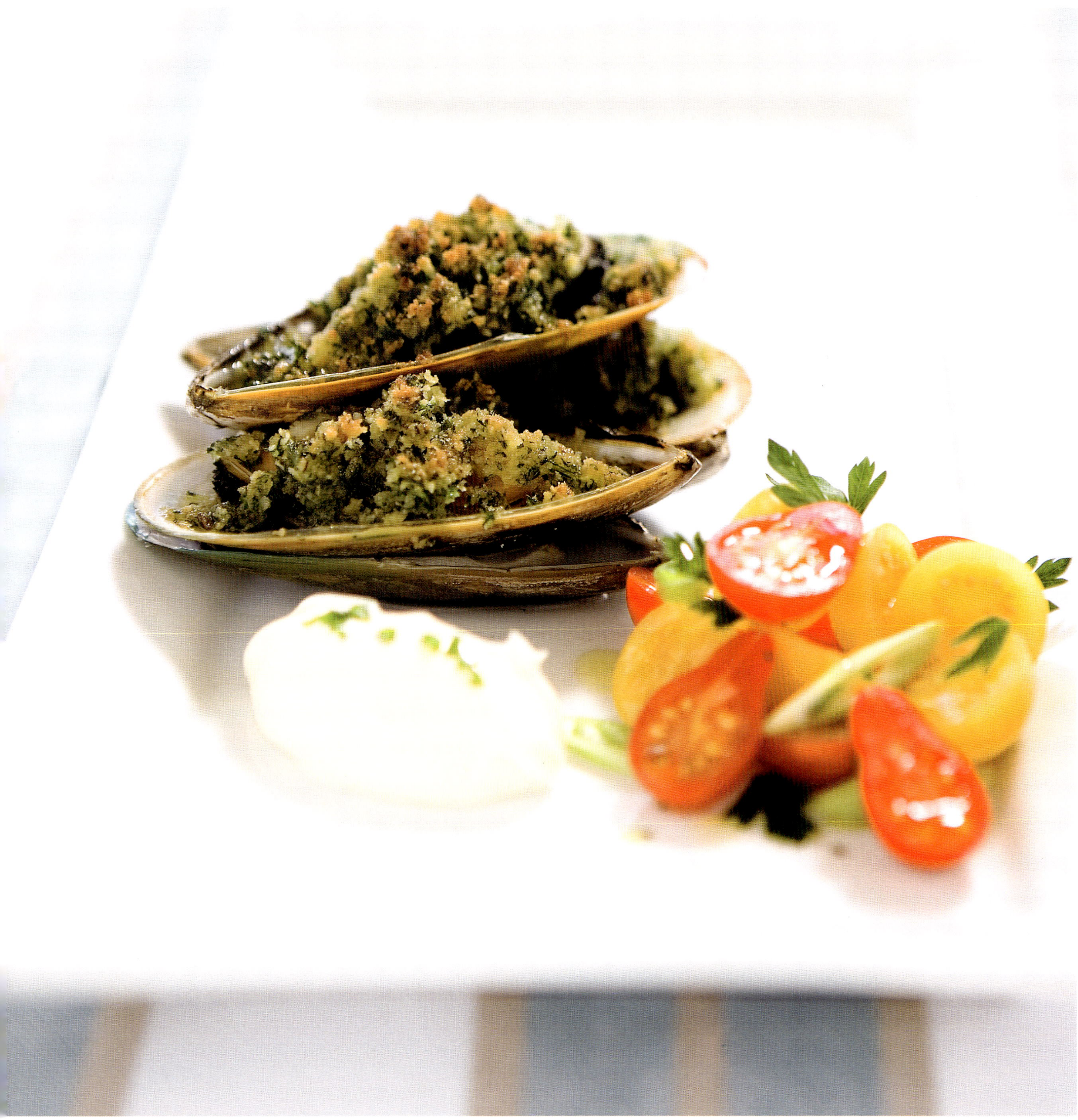

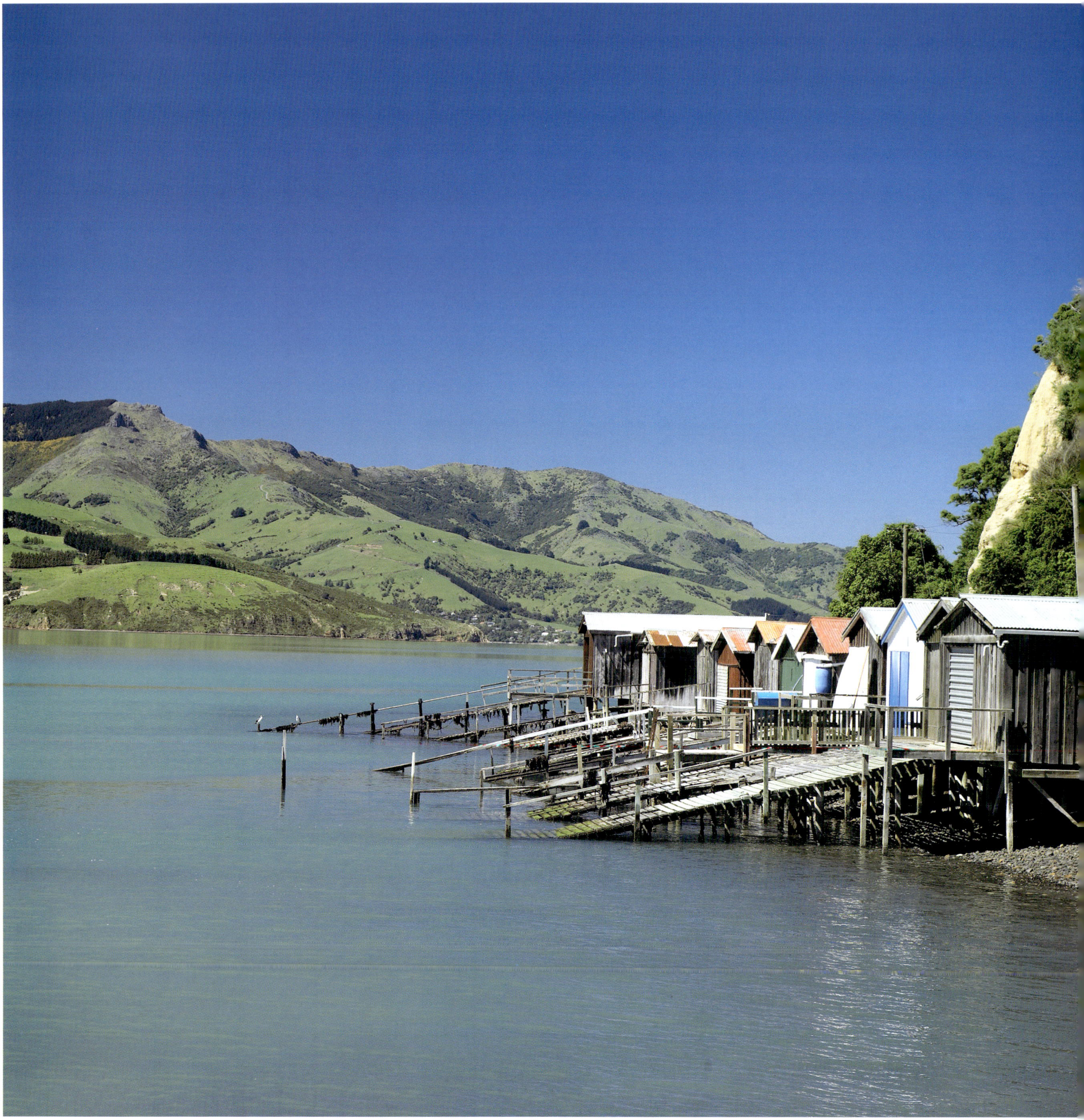

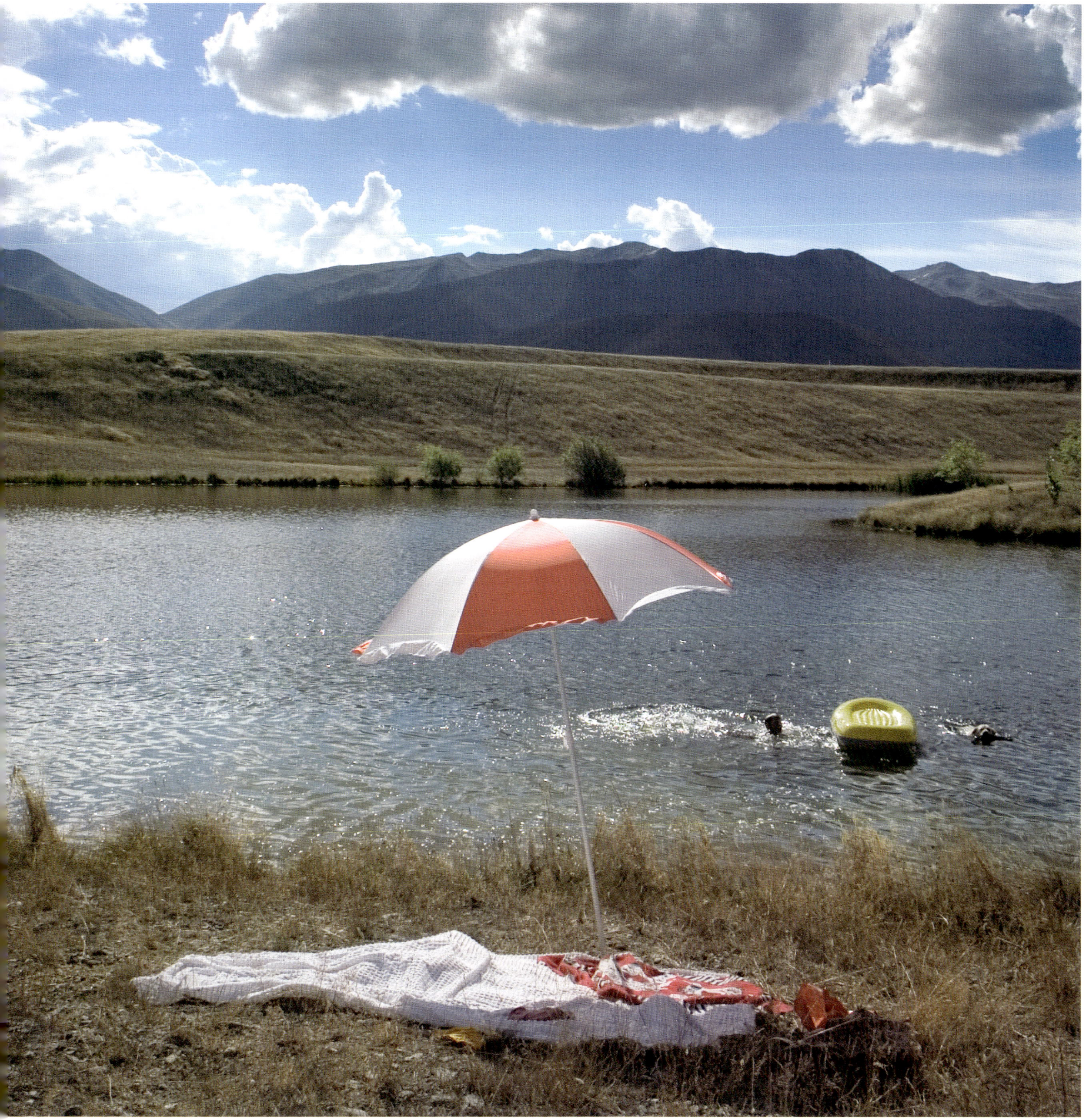

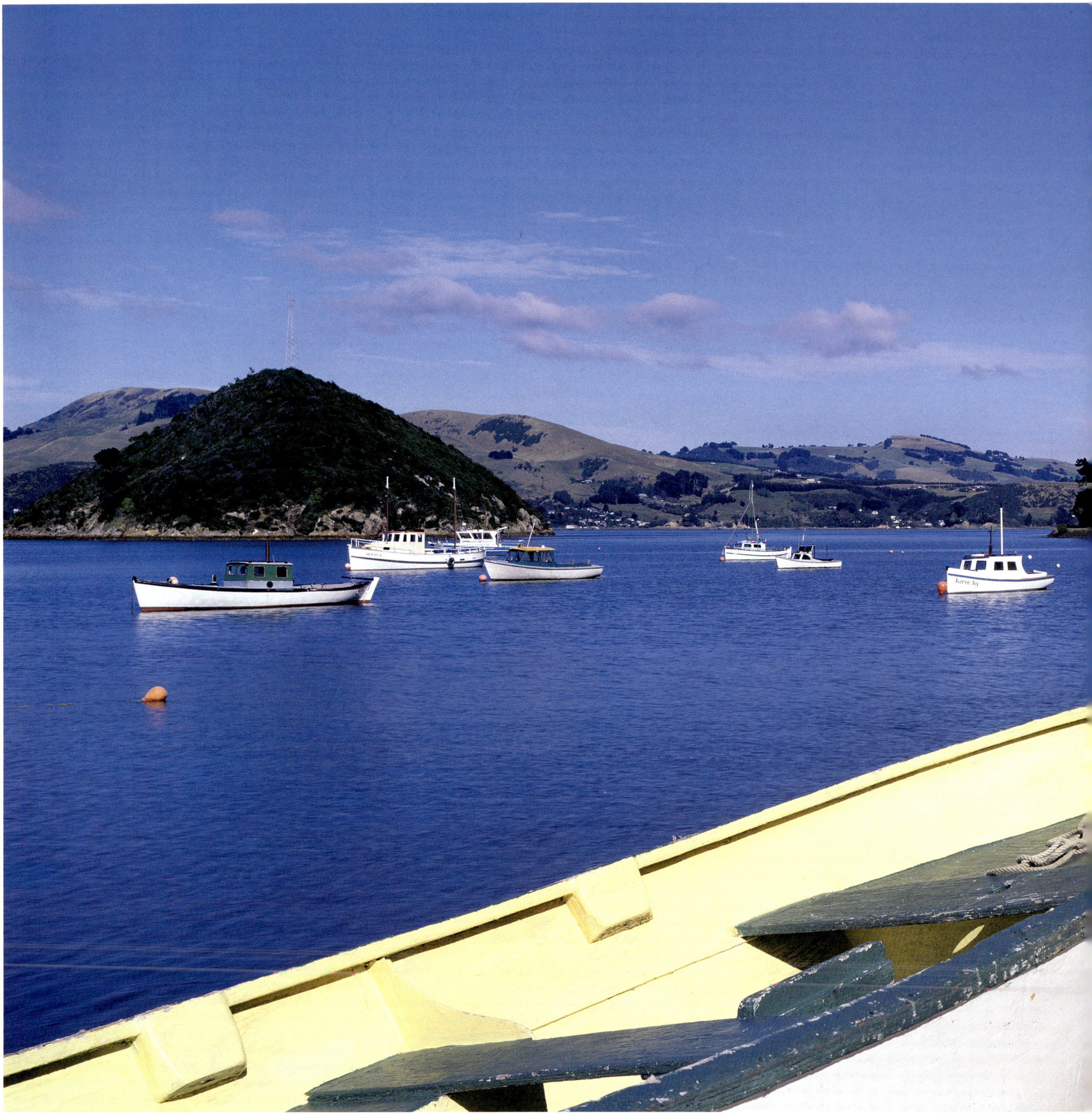

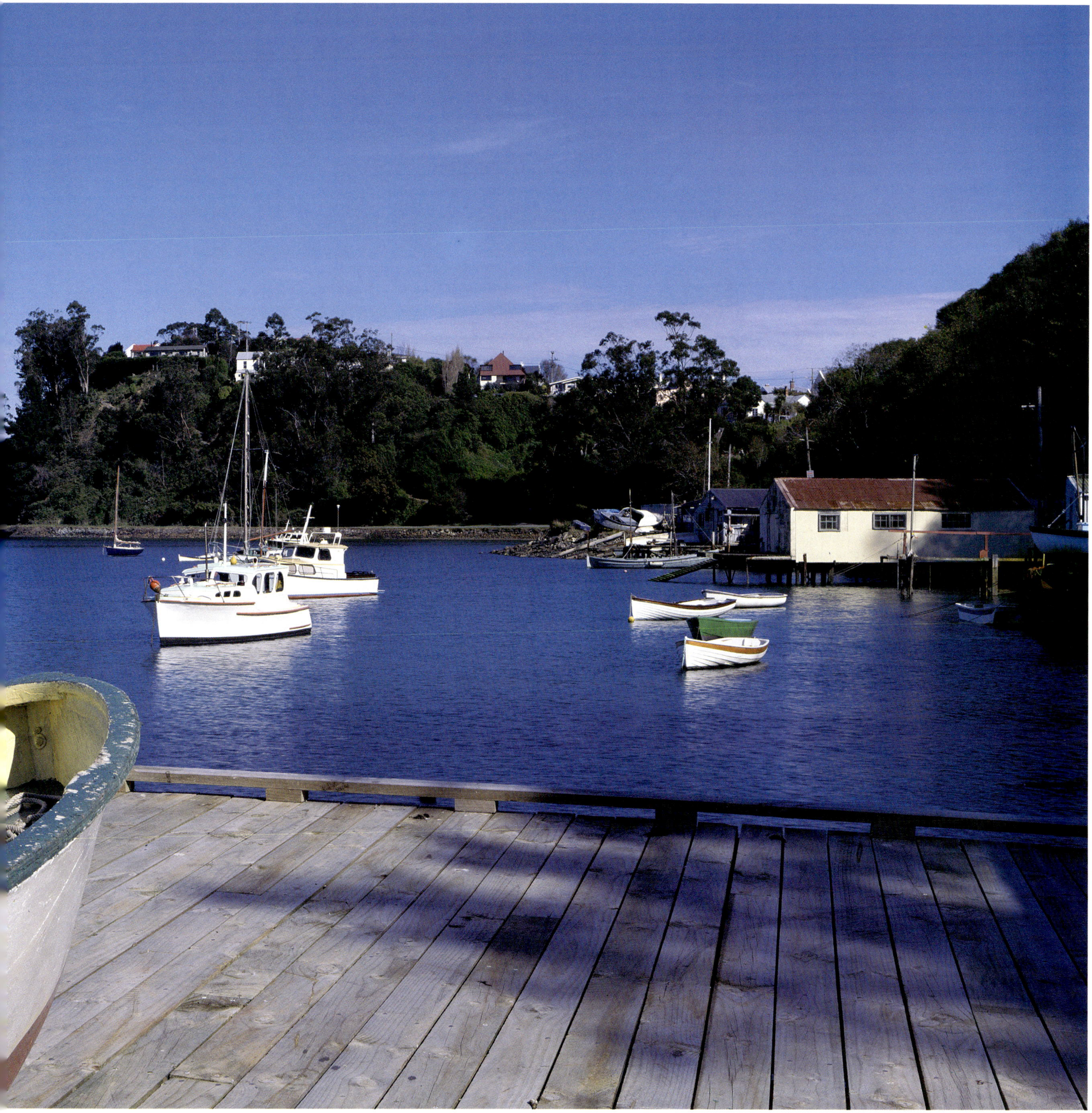

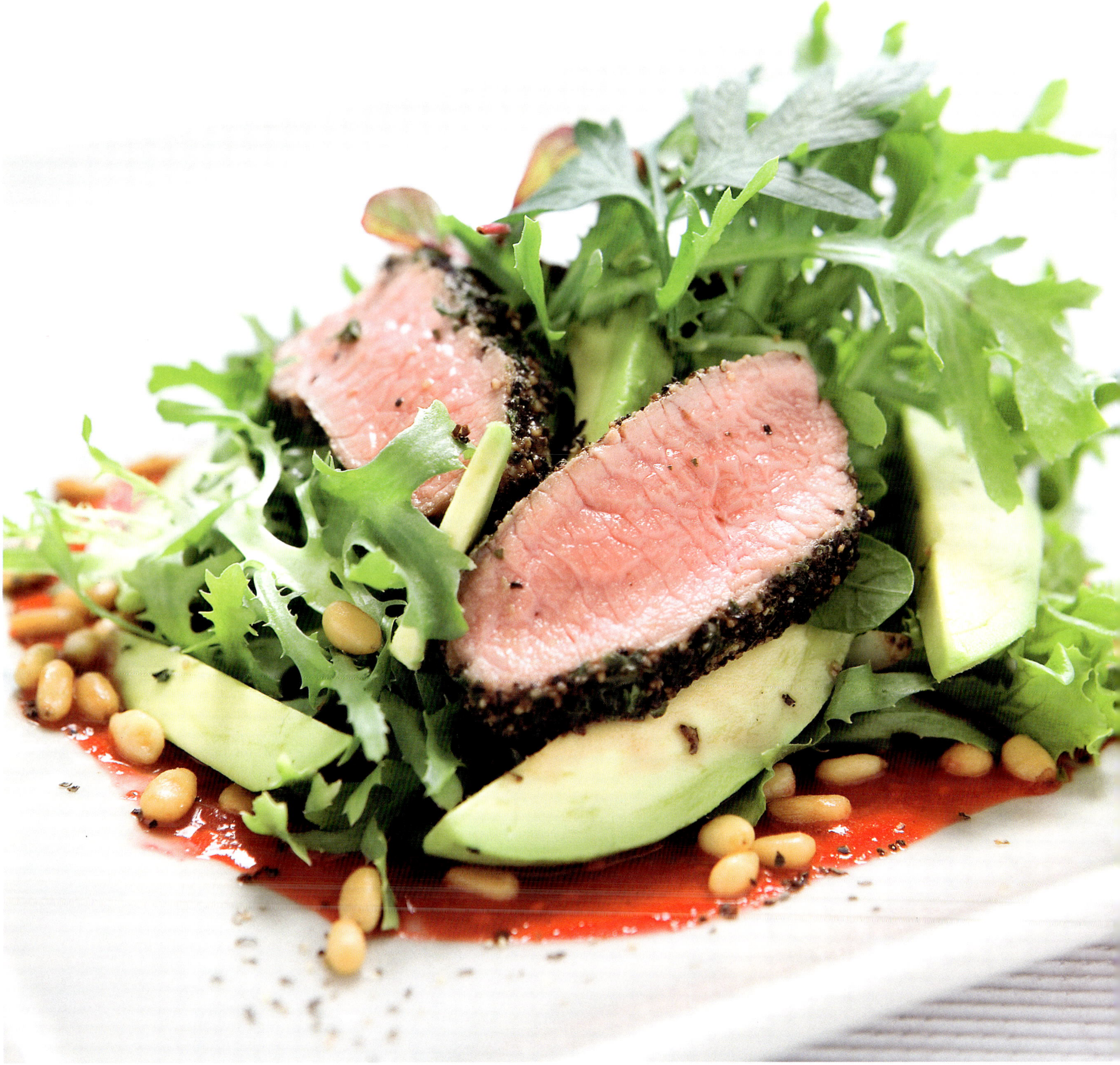

Peppered Lamb, Pine Nut and Avocado Salad with Raspberry Dressing

Serves 4

Ingredients

4 tbsp cracked black pepper
1 tsp salt
2 tbsp chopped parsley
2 lamb short loins
5 tbsp vegetable oil
3 tbsp pine nuts
salt
salad leaves
1 avocado, peeled and sliced

Raspberry Dressing

1 cup frozen raspberries, defrosted and drained
1 tbsp white wine vinegar
2 tbsp sugar
2 tbsp vegetable oil
salt and pepper

Make the Raspberry Dressing and set aside.
Mix together black pepper, salt and parsley. Roll the lamb in the mix to coat well and set aside.
Heat 3 tbsp oil in a small frying pan to a medium heat. Cook the pine nuts, keeping them moving until golden brown. Drain and sprinkle with a little salt.
Heat 2 tbsp oil in a separate frying pan to a medium to low heat. Cook the lamb for approximately 3–4 minutes on each side. Remove from frying pan and rest the meat, covered, for 4 minutes.
Slice each piece of lamb into 6–8 slices.

To make the Raspberry Dressing

Blend raspberries, vinegar, sugar and oil together well. Strain. Season with salt and pepper to taste.

Assembly

Place 2–3 tbsp Raspberry Dressing on each plate. Top with a handful of salad leaves and a quarter of the avocado slices. Sprinkle with pine nuts. Place 3–4 slices of lamb on each salad.

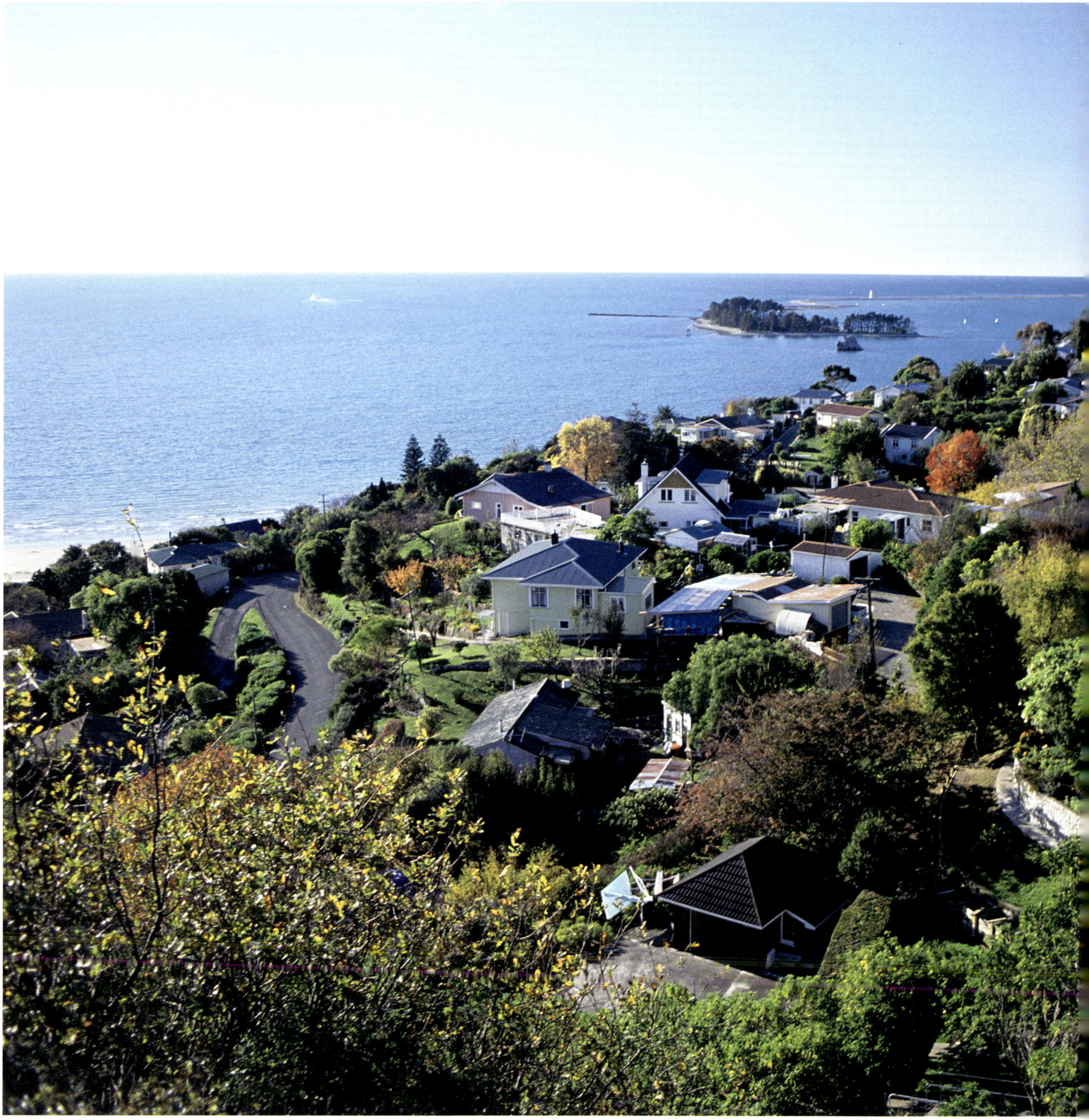

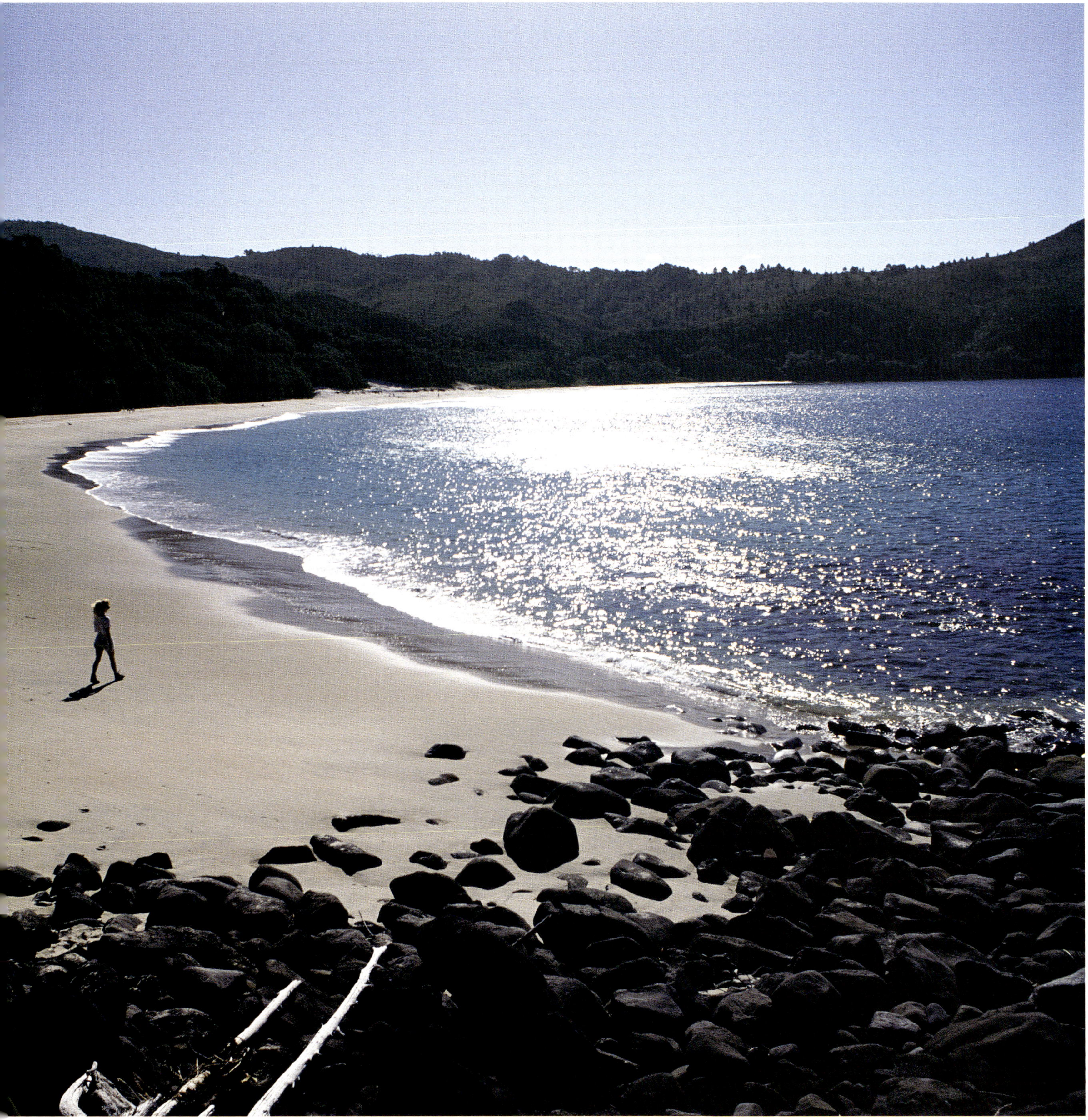

Scallop, Bacon and Pawpaw Salad with Tarragon Dressing

Serves 4

Ingredients
8 slices streaky bacon
2 cups pawpaw, peeled, cut into
  4-cm pieces
3 tomatoes, deseeded, cut into
  2-cm pieces
4 cups baby spinach leaves
1 spring onion, finely sliced
4 tbsp oil
salt and pepper
20 scallops

Tarragon Dressing
1 tsp finely chopped tarragon
1 tbsp white wine vinegar
1 tsp sugar
3 tbsp canola oil
salt and pepper to taste

Prepare the Tarragon Dressing and set aside.
Heat oven to 200°C. Place bacon on oven tray. Cook for 10 minutes. Pat off any excess fat with a paper towel and cut into 4 cm strips.
Place bacon, pawpaw, tomatoes, spinach leaves and spring onion in a large salad bowl. Add enough dressing to coat the salad.
In a large frying pan, heat enough oil to coat the entire surface, approximately 2 tbsp. Heat pan to a medium to hot heat. Sprinkle scallops with salt and pepper.
Place half the scallops in the pan. Cook for approximately 30 seconds on each side, then set aside.
Add the remaining oil and repeat the process.

To make the Tarragon Dressing
Place all ingredients in a jar with a lid and shake until mixed well.

Assembly
Divide the salad between 4 plates. Place 5 scallops on each salad and serve immediately.

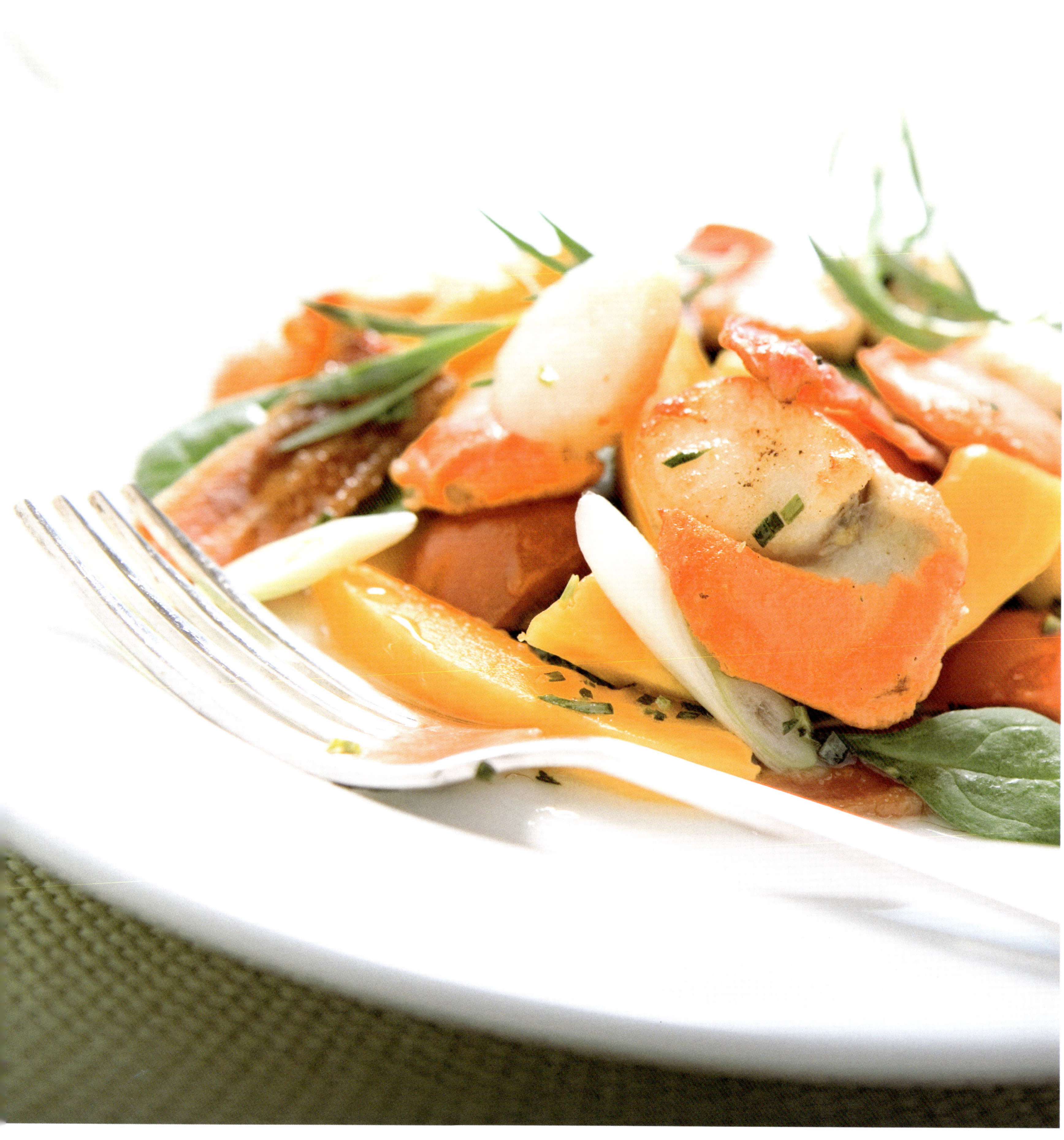

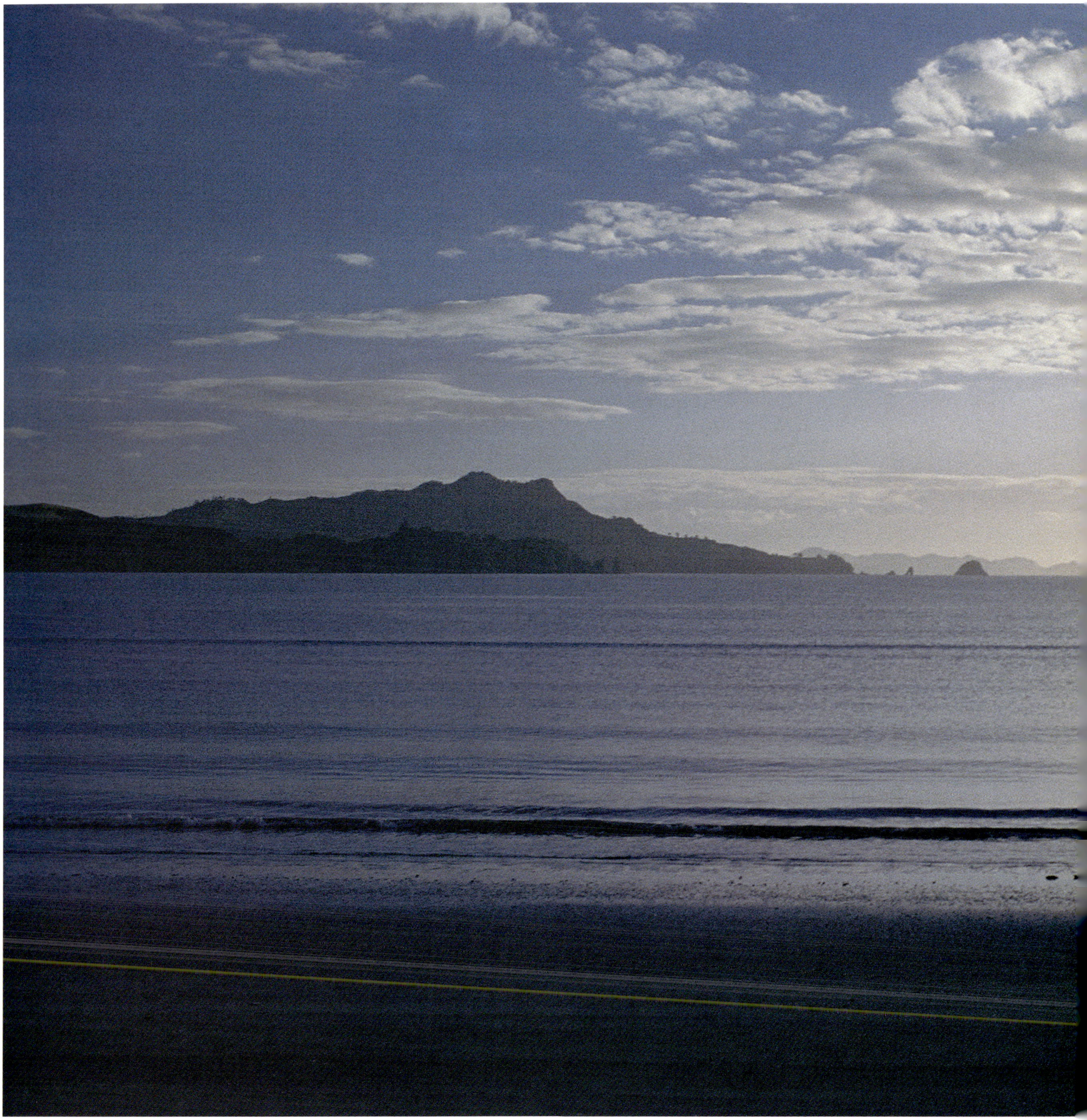

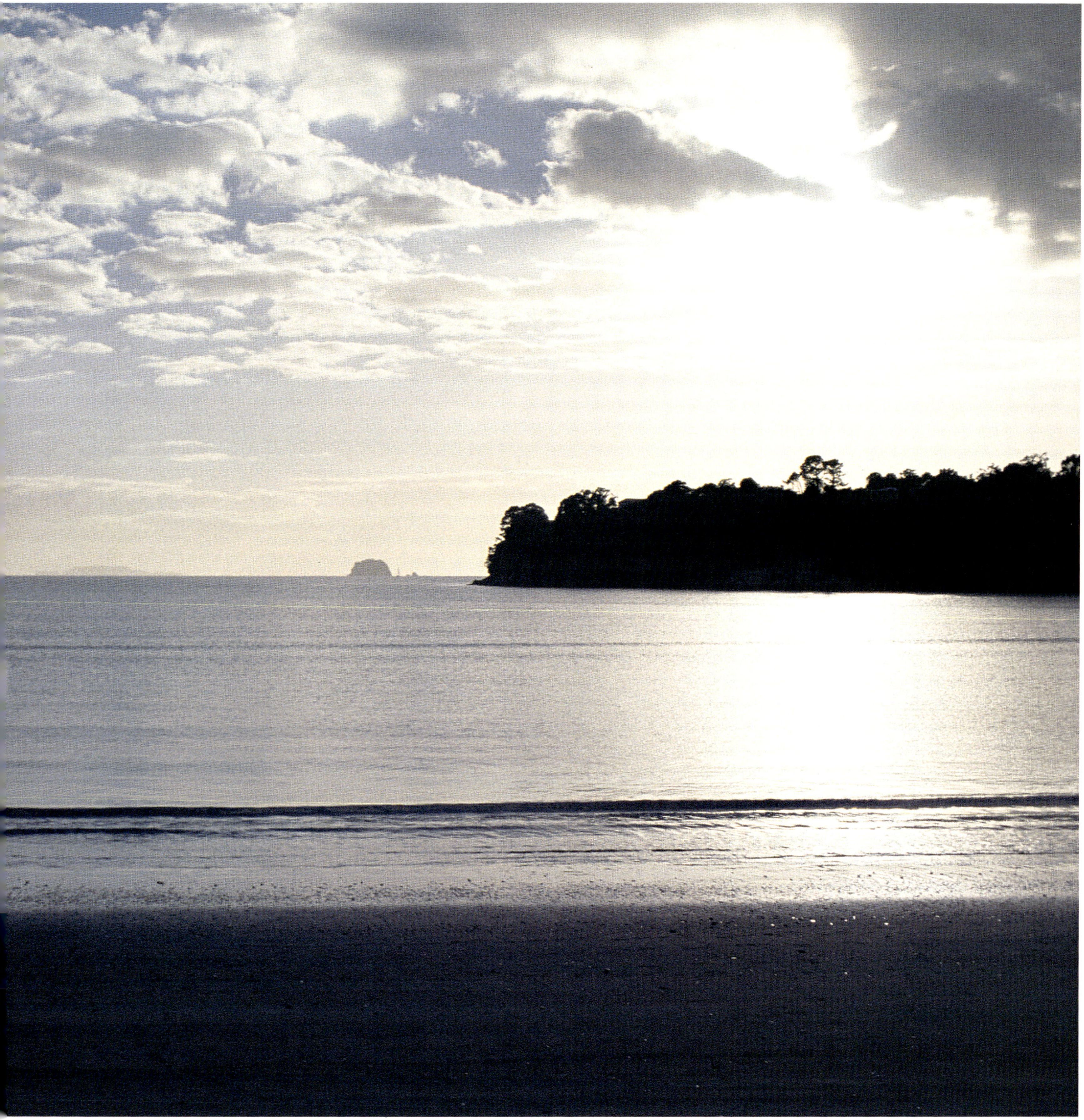

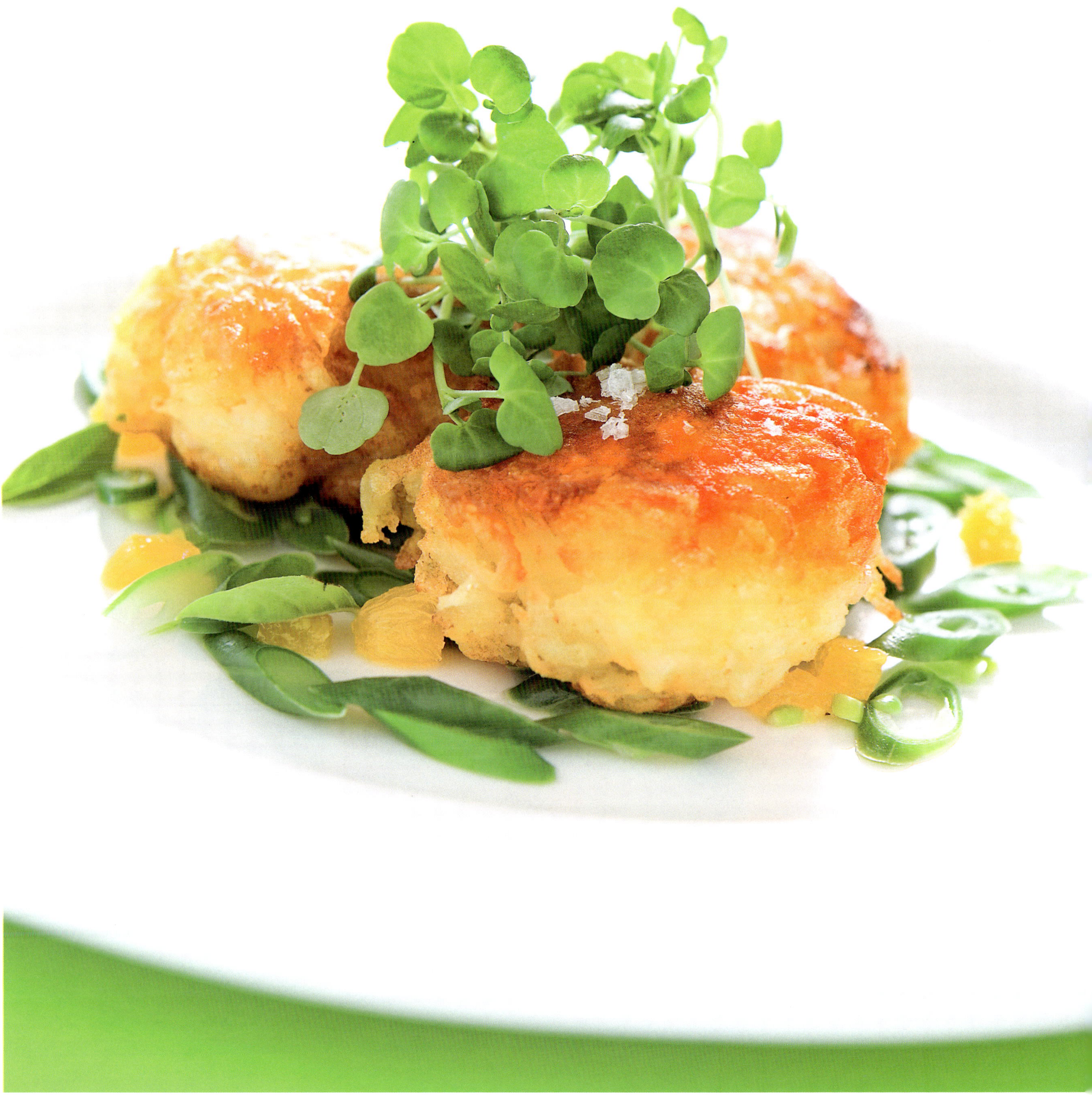

Scallops Wrapped in Crisp Potato with Green Beans, Orange and Basil Butter

Serves 4

Ingredients

12–16 scallops
3 cups boiled and grated
  Agria potatoes
salt and pepper
1 cup green beans, finely sliced
1 orange, peeled
60 ml (¼ cup) vegetable oil
baby salad leaves

Basil Butter
150 g butter
1 tbsp chopped basil
salt and pepper

Pat the scallops dry with kitchen paper.
Mix the grated potato with a little salt and pepper.
Using hands, mould the potato around each scallop.
Bring a saucepan of salted water to the boil. Add beans and cook for 30 seconds. Drain. Place beans in cold water and drain well when cool.
Segment the orange. Cut into small pieces. Mix with beans. Season with salt and pepper to taste.
Meanwhile, prepare the Basil Butter.
Heat vegetable oil in a frying pan to a medium heat. Cook the scallops until golden brown, approximately 2 minutes each side. Drain on kitchen paper. Sprinkle with salt.

To make the Basil Butter
Melt butter on a low heat. Add the basil and salt and pepper.

Assembly

Divide the bean and orange mixture between 4 plates. Divide the scallops between the plates. Top with a few baby salad leaves and drizzle with Basil Butter.

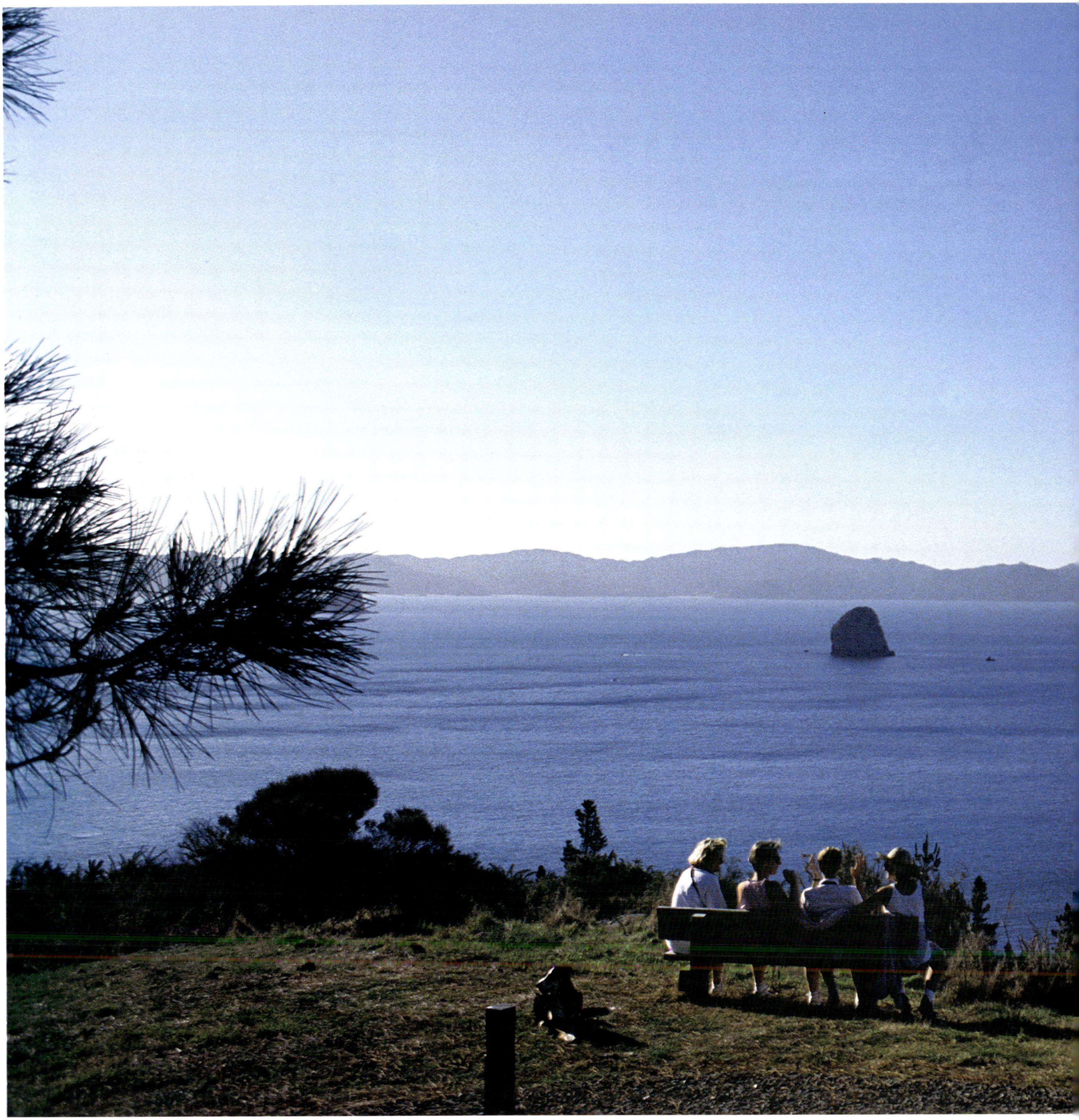

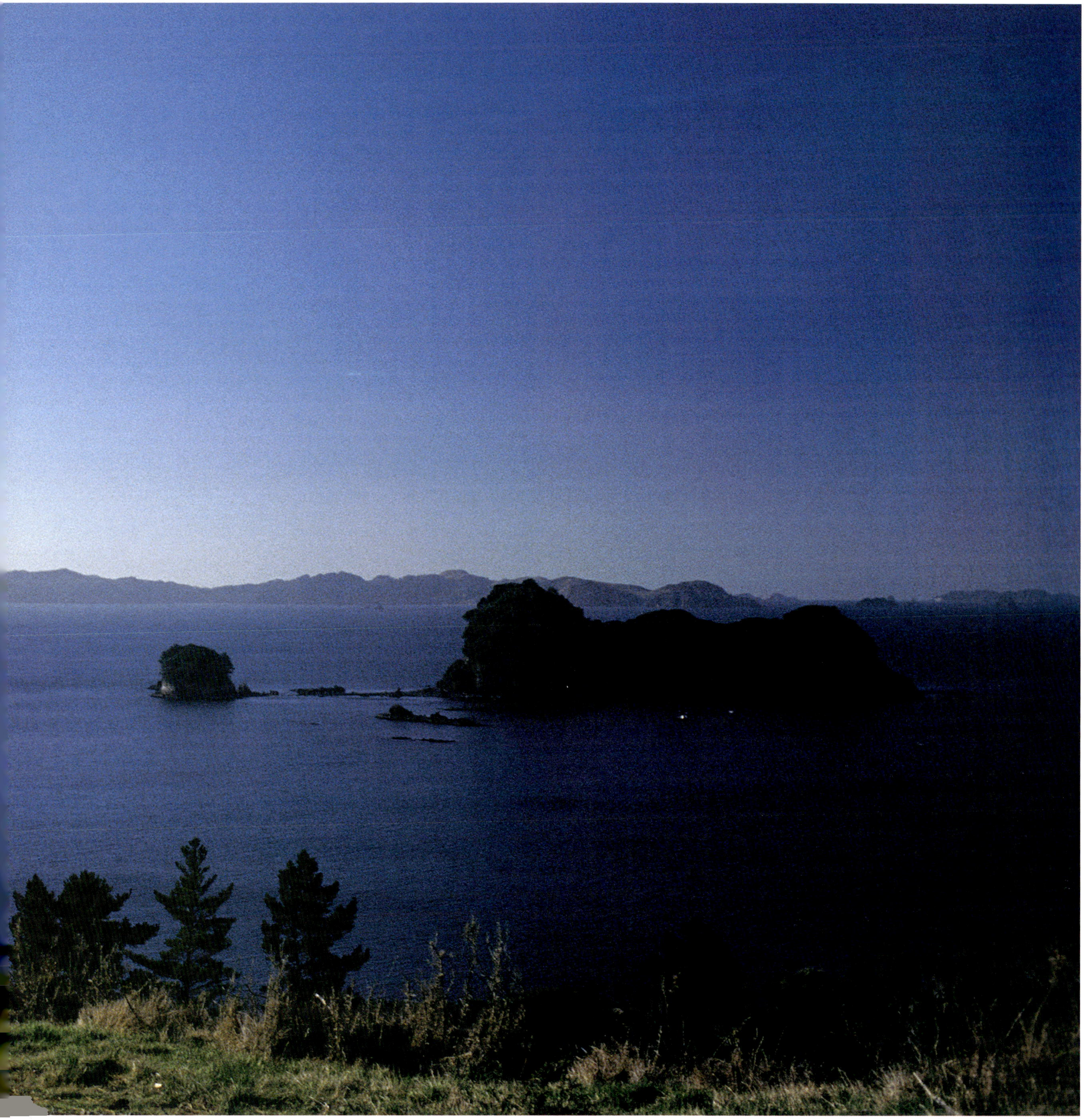

Chicken, Mango and Cashew Nut Salad with Ginger Dressing

Serves 4

Ingredients

300 g sliced smoked chicken
1 mango, peeled and sliced
¼ cup finely sliced spring onion
½ cup roasted cashew nuts
1 red capsicum, finely sliced (optional)
2 curly leaf green lettuces

Ginger Dressing
4 tbsp canola oil
2 tbsp white wine vinegar
2 tsp finely minced ginger
1 tsp sugar
1 tbsp sesame seeds
1 tbsp chopped coriander leaves
salt and pepper

Place chicken, mango, spring onion, cashew nuts and capsicum in a salad bowl. Meanwhile, make the Ginger Dressing.

Add enough dressing to coat ingredients and mix well. Gently toss through lettuce leaves, adding more dressing if required. Divide between 4 bowls or plates and serve.

To make the Ginger Dressing

Place oil, vinegar, ginger, sugar, sesame seeds and coriander in a jar with a tight-fitting lid. Shake well. Season with salt and pepper to taste.

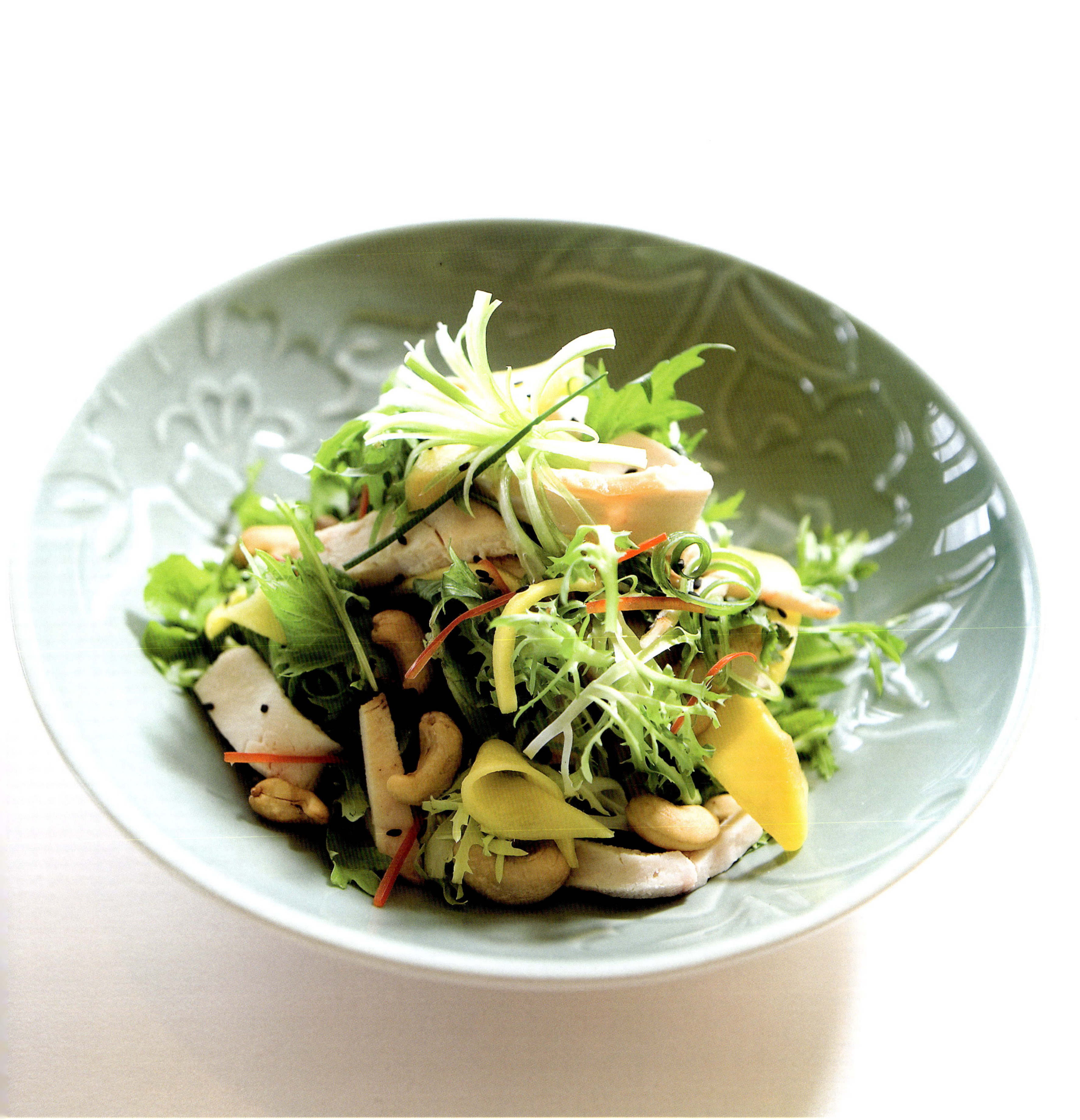

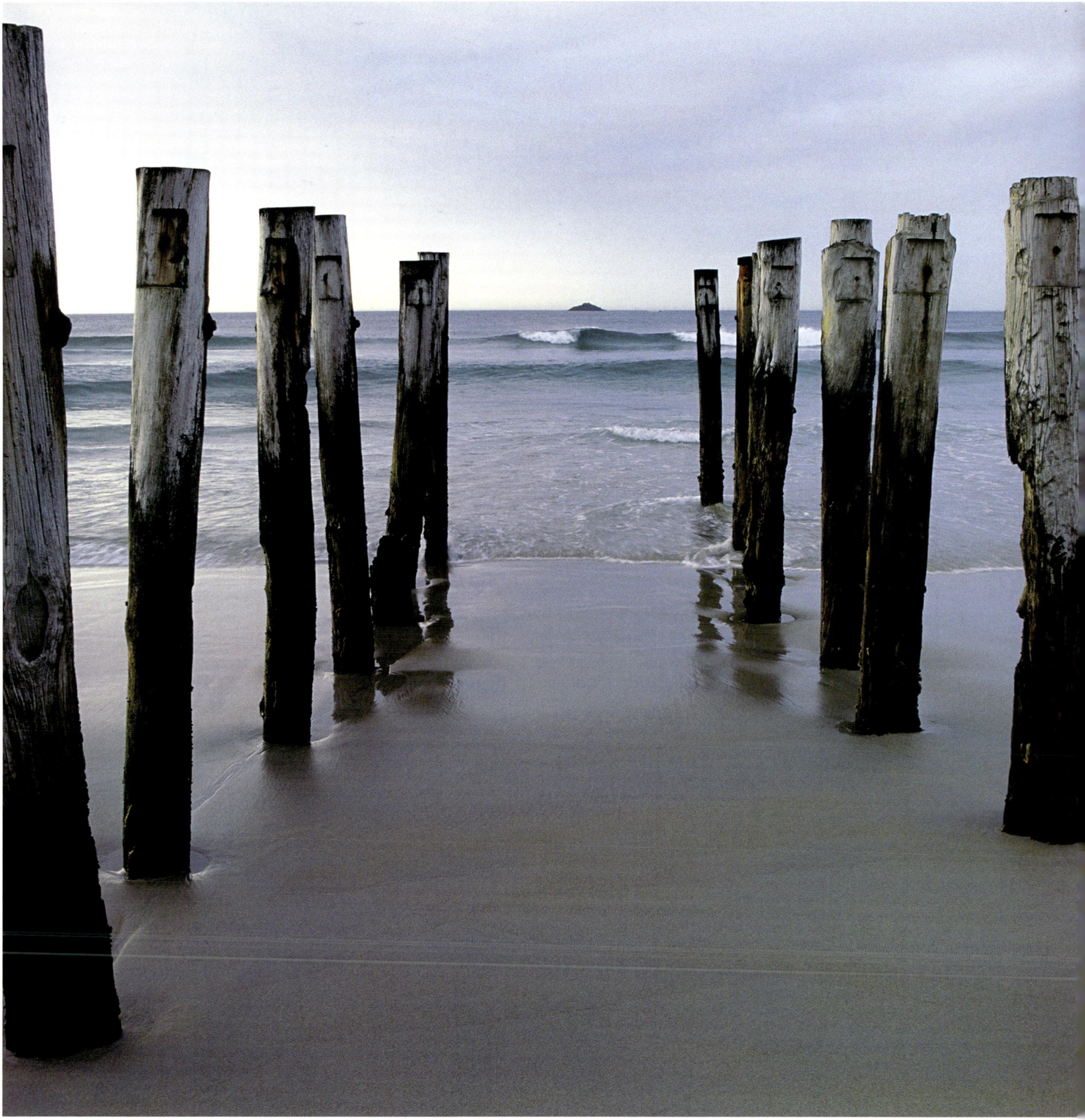

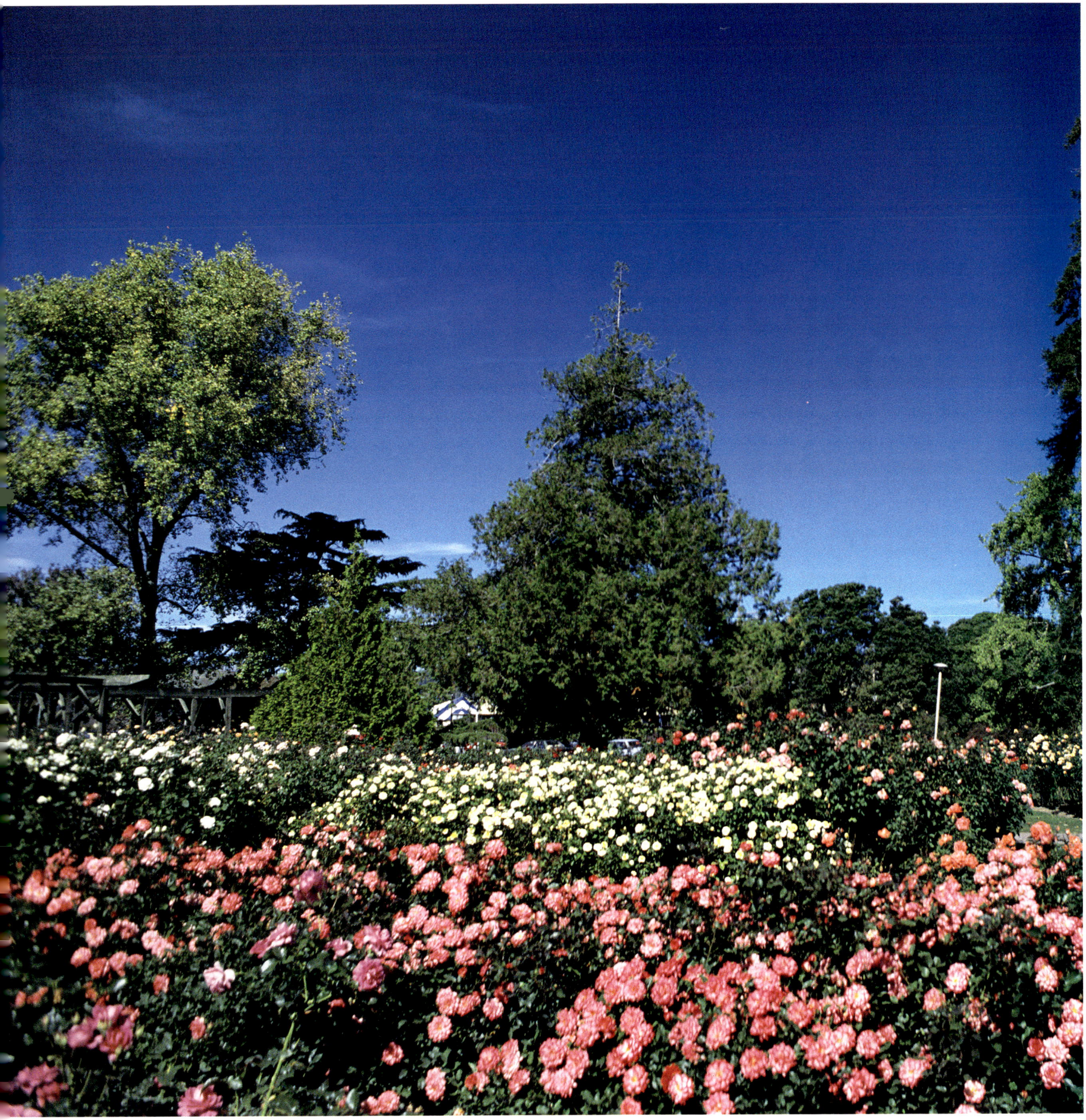

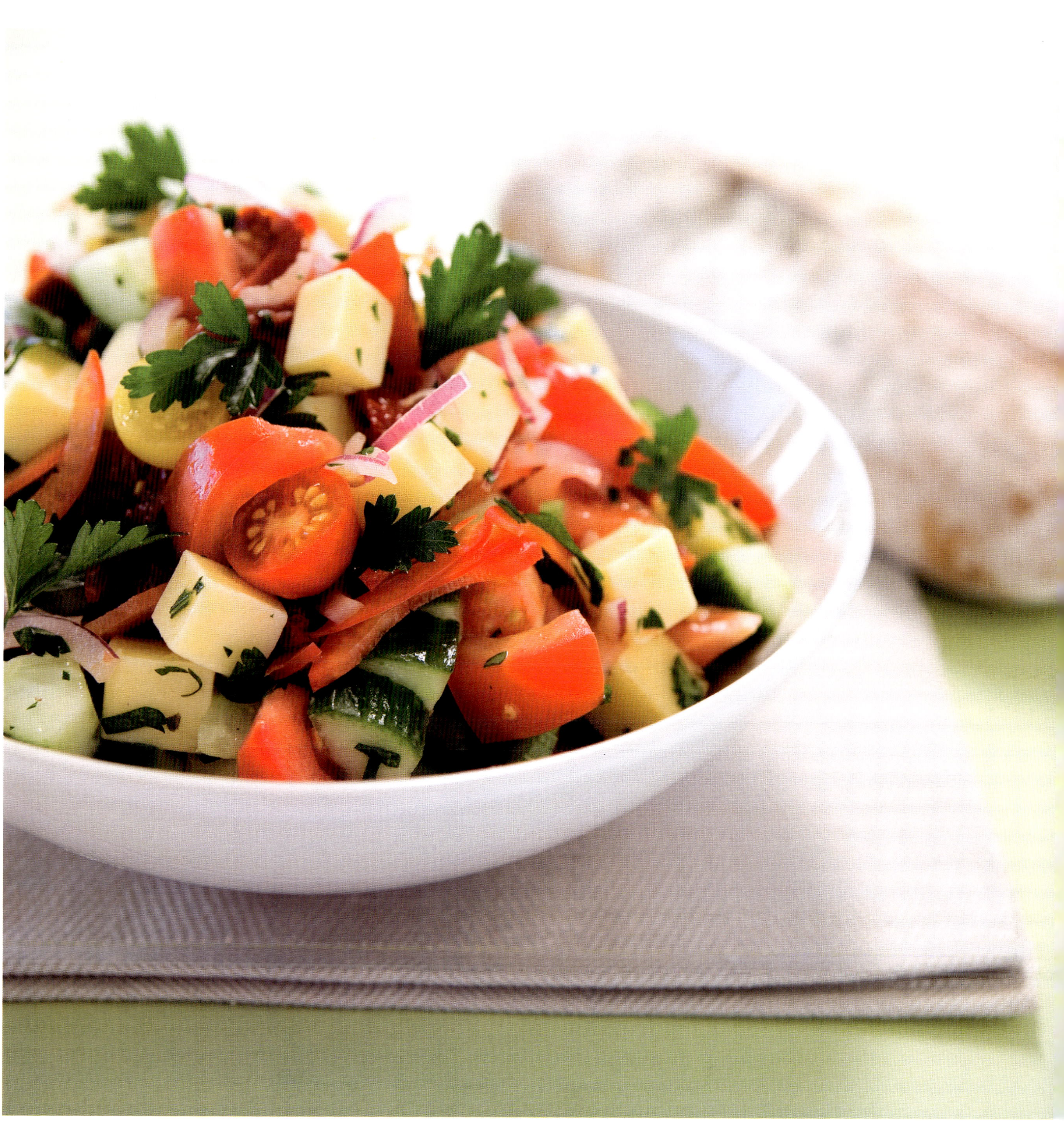

Summer Salad

Serves 6-8

Ingredients

1 telegraph cucumber, deseeded
250 g Cheddar cheese
1 small red onion, thinly sliced
2 sticks celery, thinly sliced
6 sundried tomatoes, thinly sliced
1 x 250-g punnet cherry tomatoes, cut in halves
3 medium-sized tomatoes, cut in quarters
½ cup chopped parsley
salt and pepper

Malt Vinegar Dressing
60 ml (¼ cup) malt vinegar
60 ml (¼ cup) soft brown sugar
salt and pepper

Make the Malt Vinegar Dressing and set aside.
Cut the cucumber and cheese into cubes. Place in a large salad bowl.
Add the onion, celery, sundried tomatoes, halved cherry tomatoes, quartered tomatoes and parsley.
Add the dressing. Toss gently and season with salt and pepper to taste.
Serve with good quality bread, to accompany a barbecue.

To make the Malt Vinegar Dressing
Mix together vinegar and sugar. Season with salt and pepper to taste.

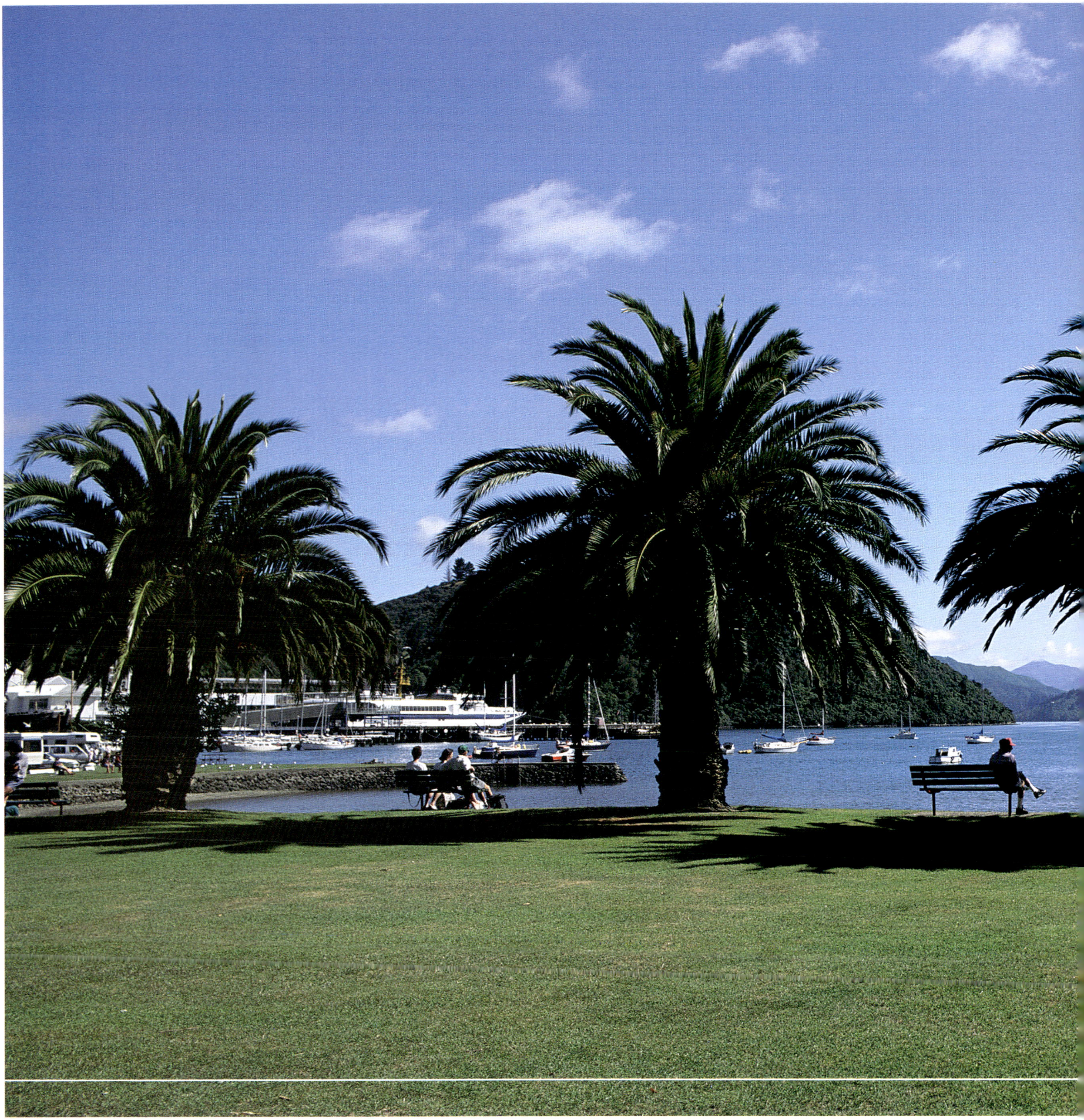

Dessert

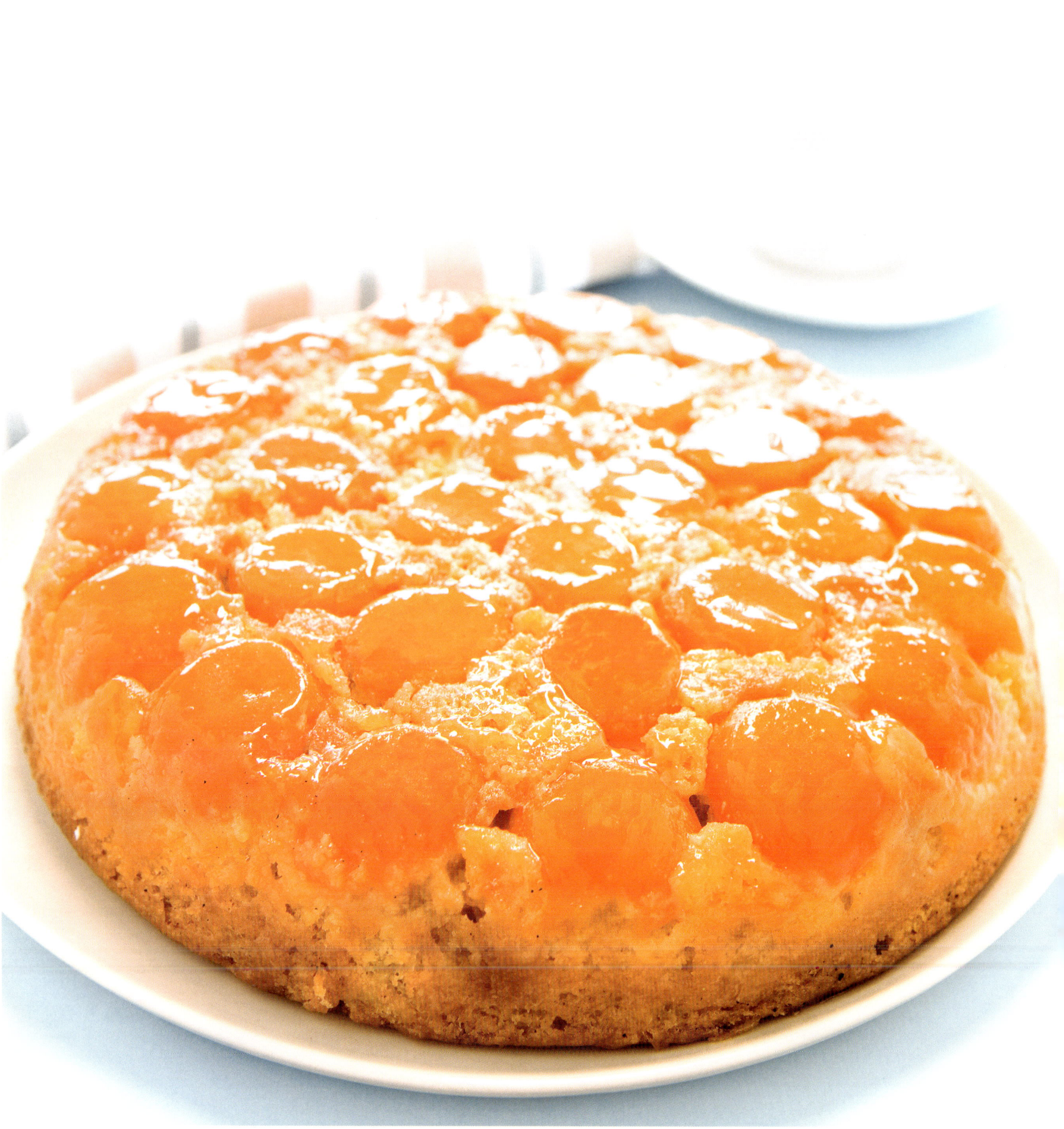

Apricot Cake

Ingredients

185 g butter
¾ cup soft brown sugar
14–17 apricots, halved
2 cups flour
1 tsp baking soda
1 tsp baking powder
½ tsp salt
1 cup sugar
2 tsp vanilla essence
2 eggs
250 ml (1 cup) buttermilk

Preheat oven to 175°C.

Melt 60 g butter in a 25-cm cast-iron skillet on a low heat. Sprinkle with soft brown sugar and leave for 3 minutes.

Arrange apricots, cut side up, to cover bottom of the skillet.

Into a bowl, sift together flour, baking soda, baking powder and salt. Set aside.

In a separate bowl, cream together 125 g butter and sugar. Add vanilla, then eggs, one at a time. Add buttermilk, then dry ingredients. Mix well.

Gently spoon mixture over apricots.

Bake for approximately 1 hour or until a toothpick inserted comes out clean.

To remove, run a knife around the side of the cake and turn out onto a plate fruit-side up. Serve with cream, vanilla ice cream or crème fraîche.

Either fresh or tinned apricot halves can be used. If using tinned apricots, drain well and dry on kitchen paper.

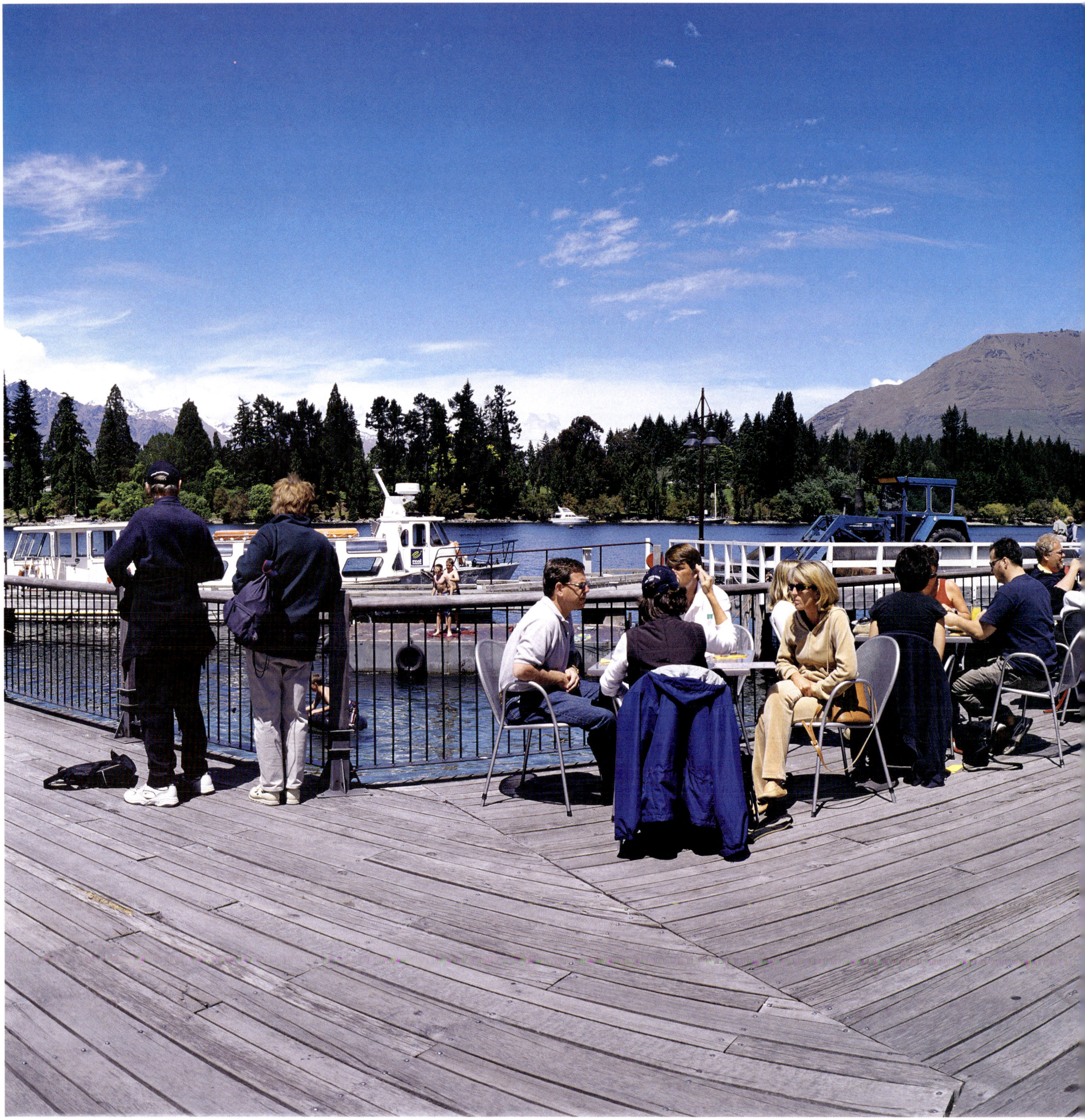

Vittoria Coffee
bar DEUTZ cafe
Vittoria Coffee
Vittoria Coffee

Buttermilk Cream with Fresh Fruit and Honey

Serves 6

Ingredients

300 ml (1¼ cups) cream
¾ cup sugar
1½ tsp vanilla essence
5 tsp gelatine powder
60 ml (¼ cup) boiling water
600 ml (2½ cups) buttermilk
selection of fresh fruit
60 ml (½ cup) clear honey
icing sugar for dusting

In a heavy-based saucepan heat cream, sugar and vanilla until the sugar has dissolved.
Dissolve gelatine in boiling water. Pour into cream mixture and stir in well. Remove from the heat.
Stir in buttermilk and mix well. Strain into a bowl.
Divide mixture between 6 x 250 ml cups, cover with clingfilm and refrigerate for 4 hours or until set.

Assembly

Dip the base of each cup in hot water for 25 seconds, then turn out onto plates. Arrange fresh fruit around each Buttermilk Cream. Drizzle with honey, dust with icing sugar and serve.

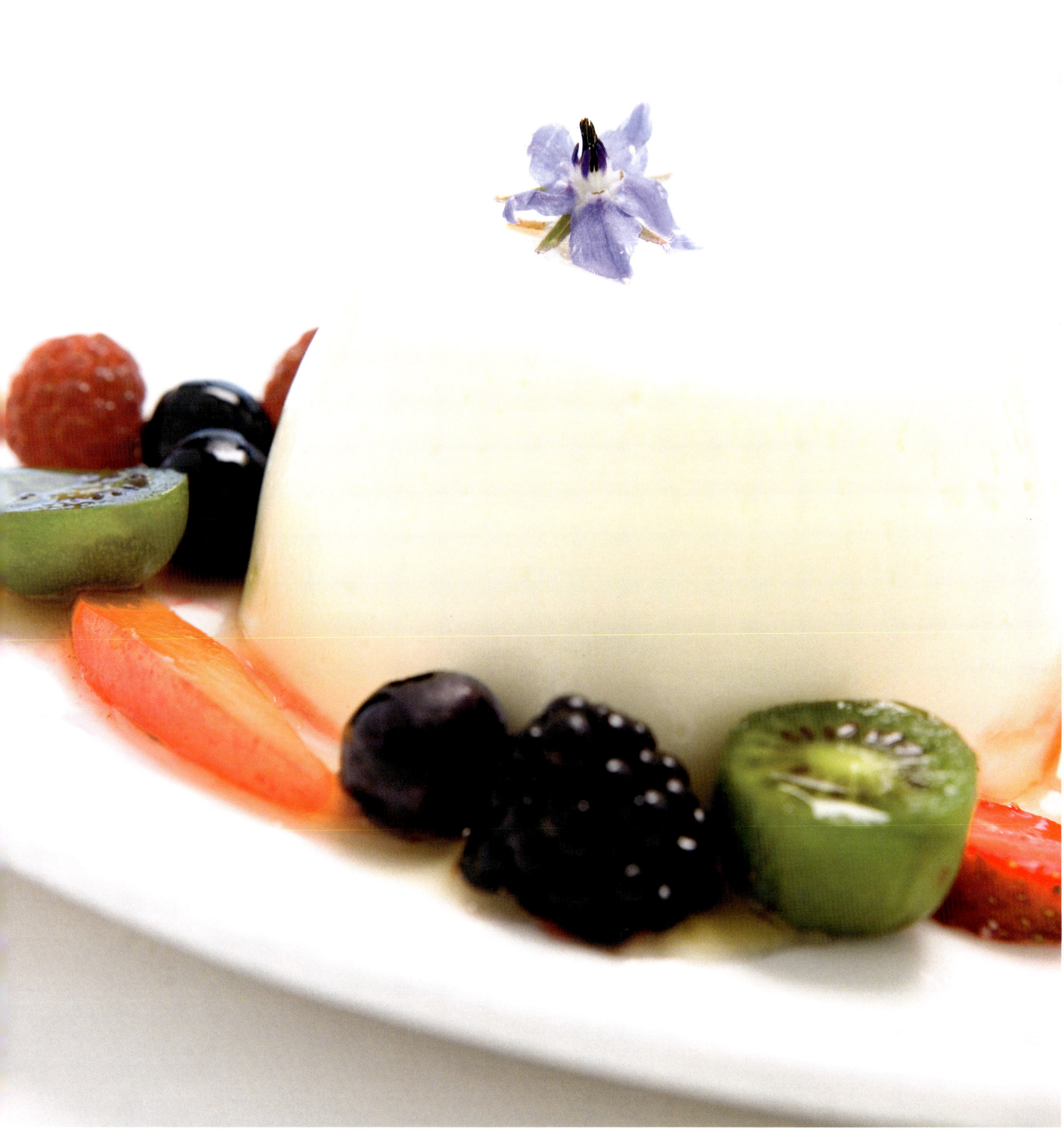

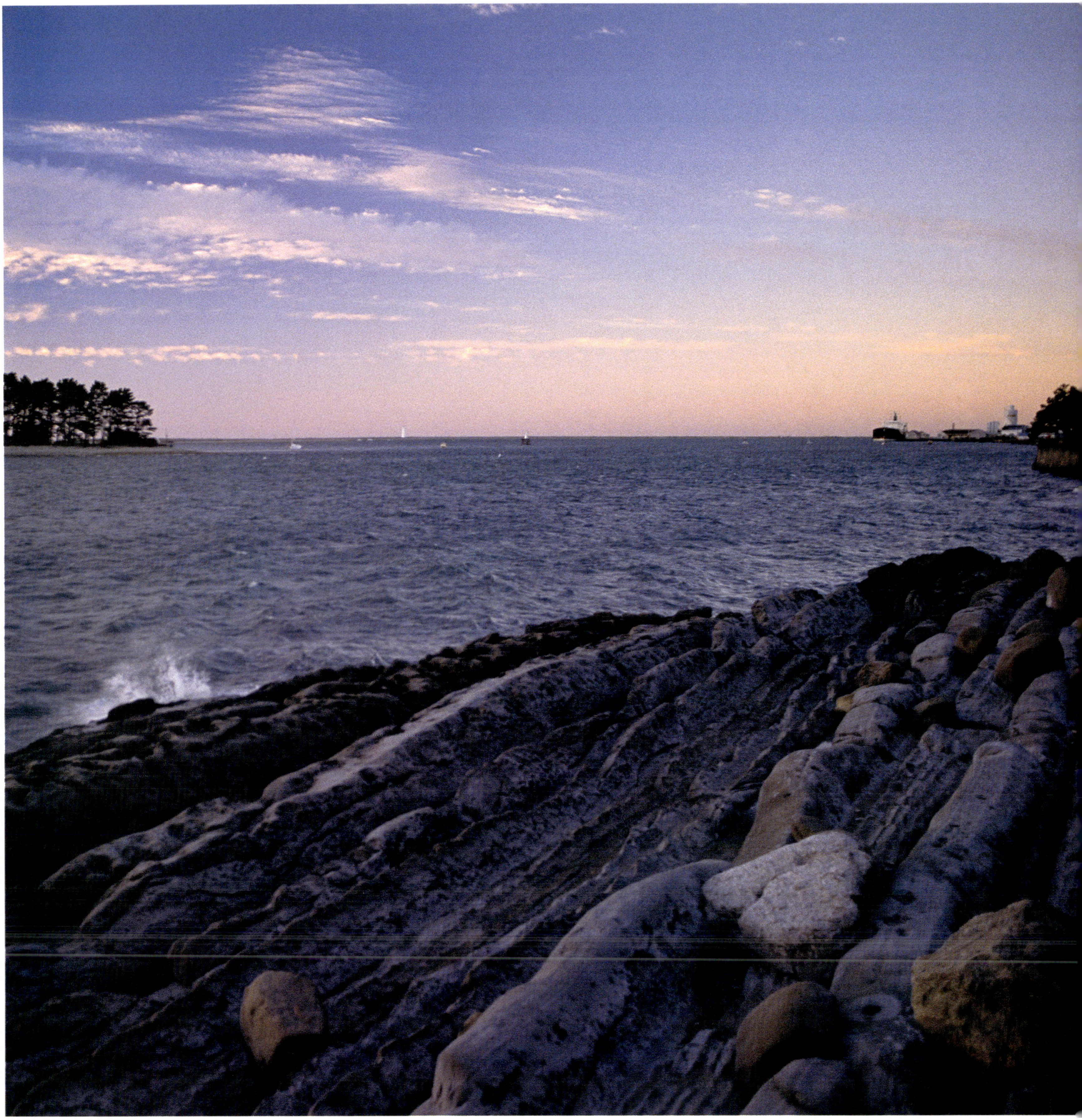

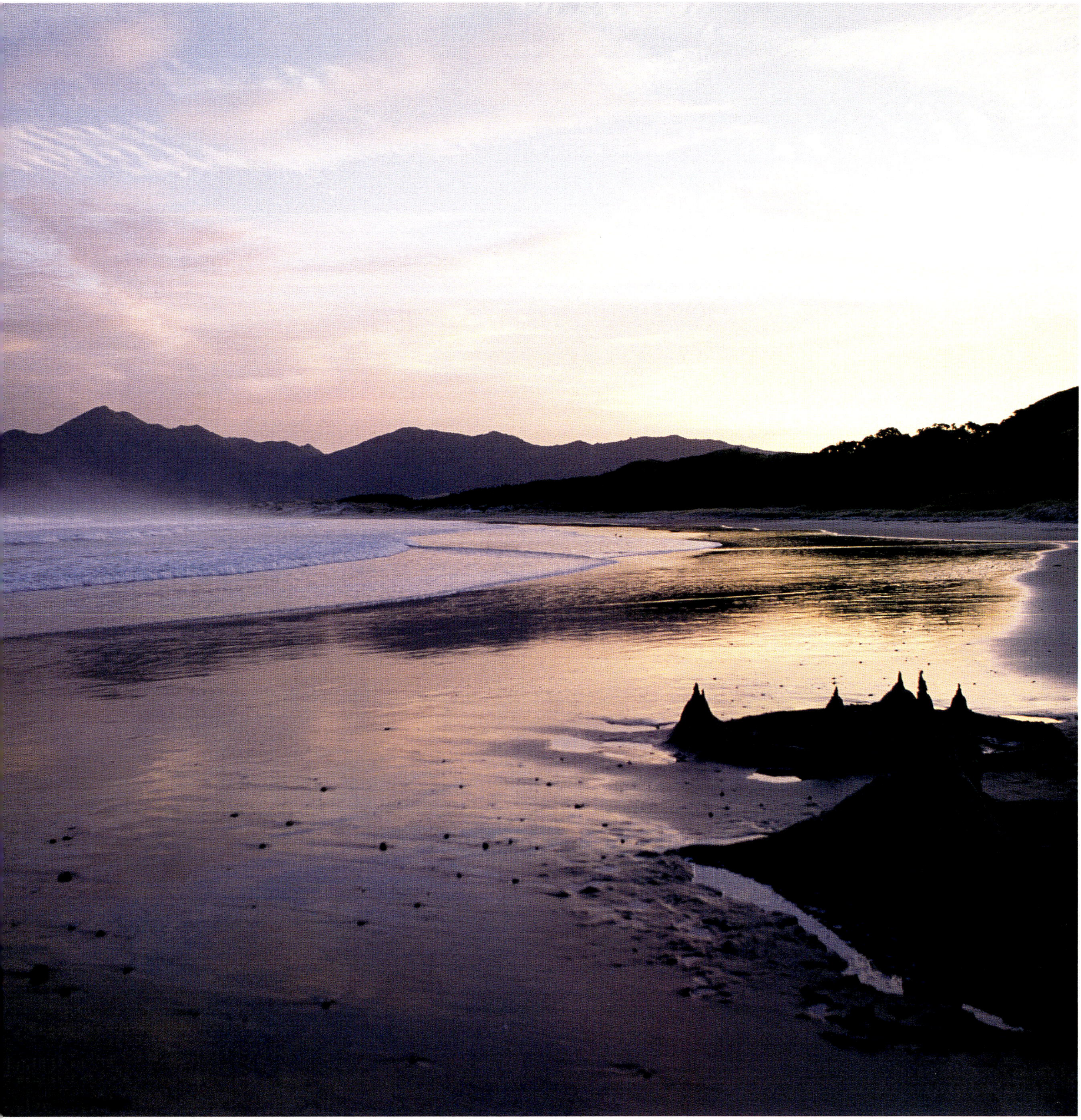

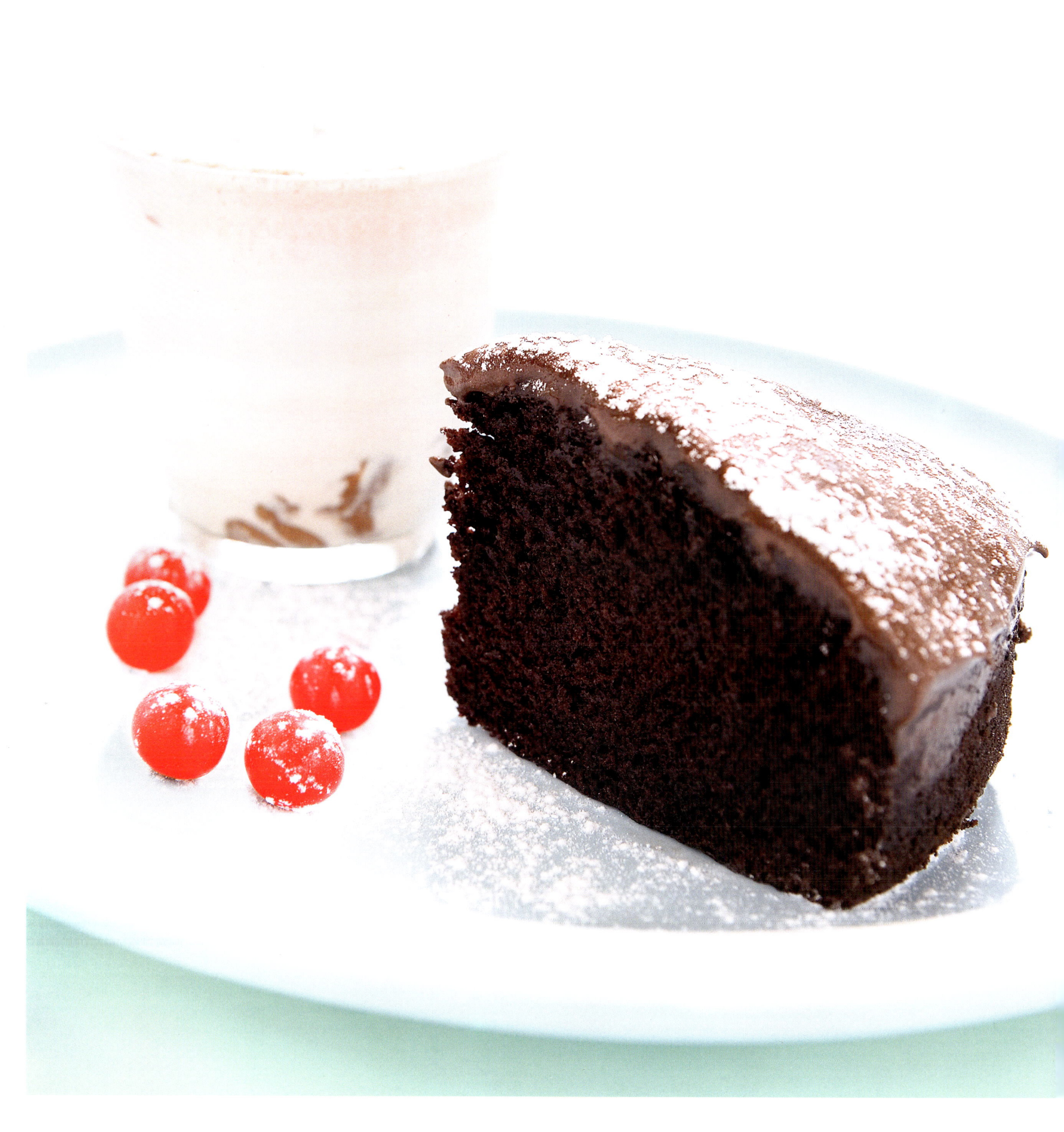

Cocoa Cake with Jaffa Shake

Shake serves 4

Ingredients

Cocoa Cake

3 cups flour
2 cups caster sugar
½ cup cocoa
2 tsp baking soda
2 tsp malt vinegar
2 tbsp vanilla essence
500 ml (2 cups) water
60 ml (¼ cup) vegetable oil

Cocoa Icing

35 g butter, softened
35 g cocoa powder
250 g icing sugar
4 tbsp milk

Jaffa Shake

500 ml (2 cups) milk
6 scoops vanilla ice cream
125 ml (½ cup) chocolate sauce
juice 1 orange

Preheat oven to 175°C.
Grease a 22-cm round cake tin and line the bottom with buttered paper.
Combine flour, sugar, cocoa, baking soda, vinegar, vanilla, water and oil. Mix well.
Pour mixture into prepared tin. Bake for 1 hour 10 minutes. Allow to rest for 10 minutes, then turn out onto a baking rack.
When cool, coat evenly with Cocoa Icing.

To make the Cocoa Icing
Cream butter until pale. Add cocoa and icing sugar. Mix well. Add milk and beat well until smooth.

To make the Jaffa Shake
Blend all ingredients together until smooth and frothy. Divide into 4 x 250 ml glasses. Serve with a slice of Cocoa Cake.

DESSERT

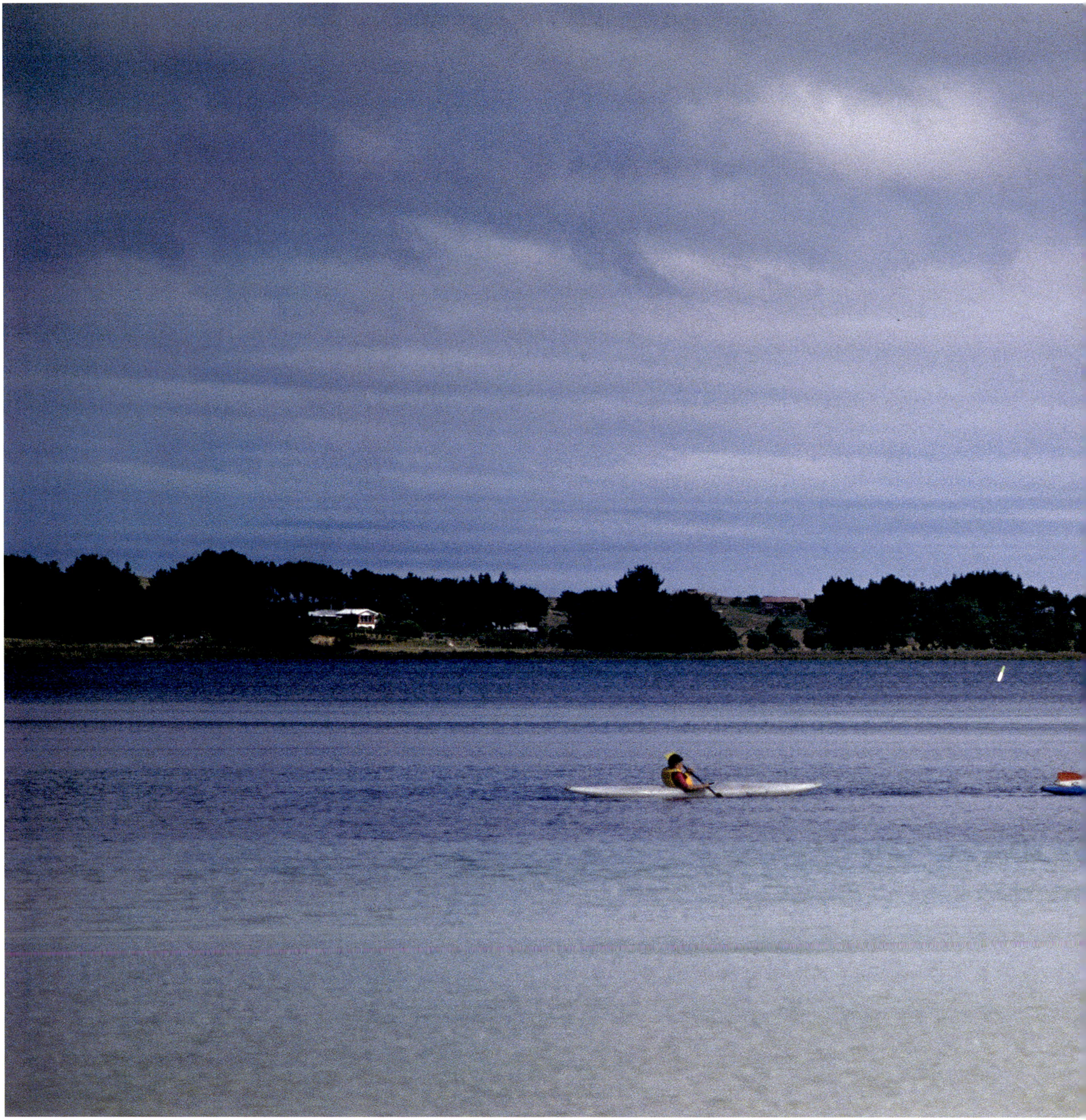

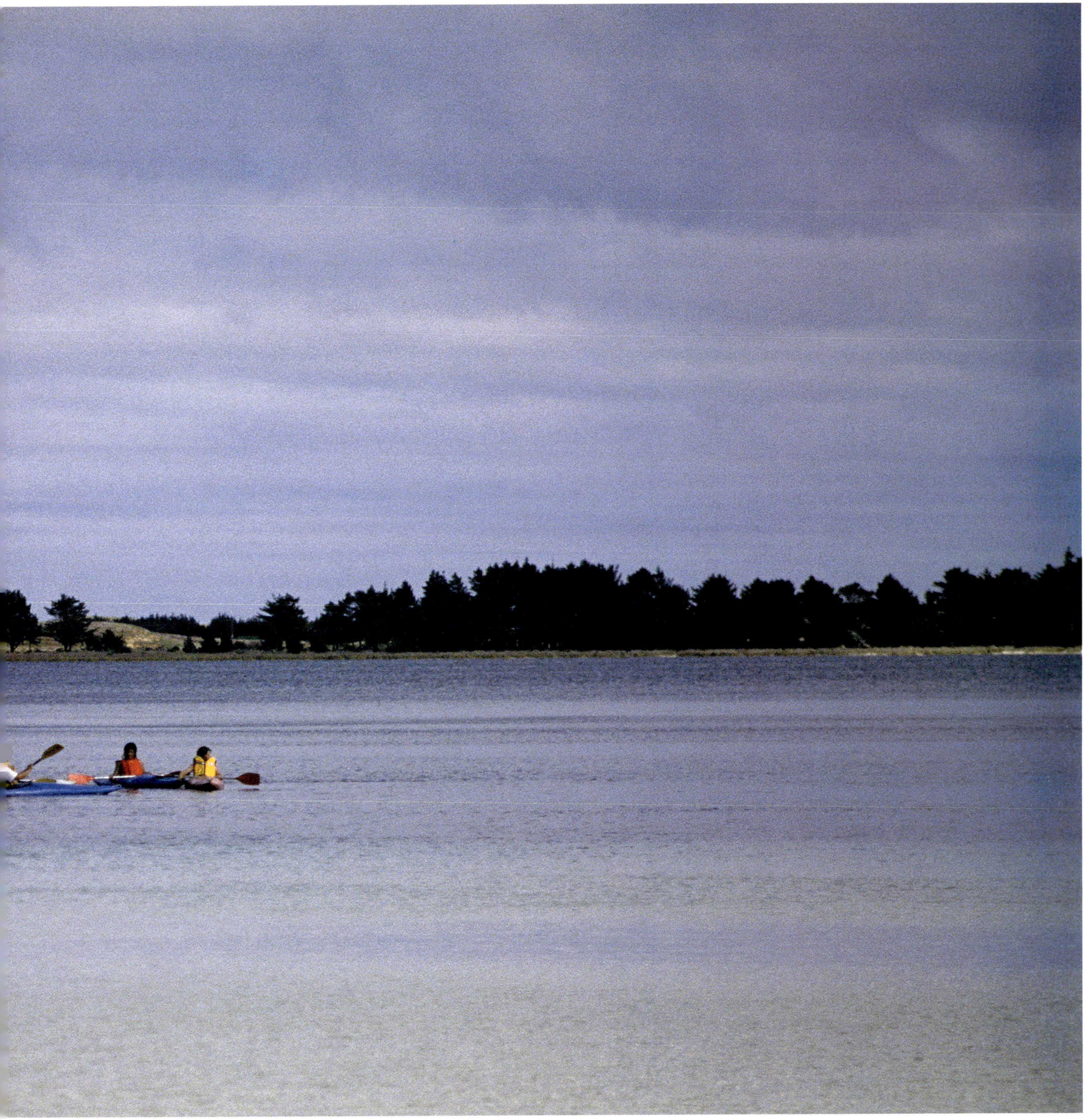

Coconut Pikelets with Banana, Bacon and Maple Syrup

Serves 4, makes 12–14 pikelets

Ingredients

1½ cups flour
3 tsp baking powder
½ tsp salt
½ cup desiccated coconut, lightly toasted
3 tbsp sugar
3 eggs, lightly beaten
375 ml (1½ cups) coconut cream
8 slices streaky bacon
50 g butter for cooking
2 bananas, peeled and sliced
250 ml (1 cup) good quality maple syrup
4 tbsp sour cream
icing sugar (optional)

Preheat oven to 180°C.

Sift together flour, baking powder and salt. Add coconut, sugar, eggs and coconut cream. Whisk until smooth.

Place bacon on a baking tray. Cook in oven for approximately 10 minutes, or until crisp. Cut slices into 3.

Brush a frying pan with butter. Bring to a medium heat, taking care not to brown the butter.

Spoon approximately 2 tbsp of mixture per pikelet into frying pan. Cook for 1 minute or until the top of pikelet starts to bubble. Turn pikelet and cook for another 30 seconds approximately.

Make 4 stacks of pikelets on an oven tray. Divide sliced banana and bacon between the layers of pikelets. Drizzle each layer with a little maple syrup. Place in oven for approximately 4 minutes to reheat.

Assembly

Top each pikelet stack with 1 tbsp sour cream. Drizzle with a little more maple syrup. Dust with icing sugar and serve.

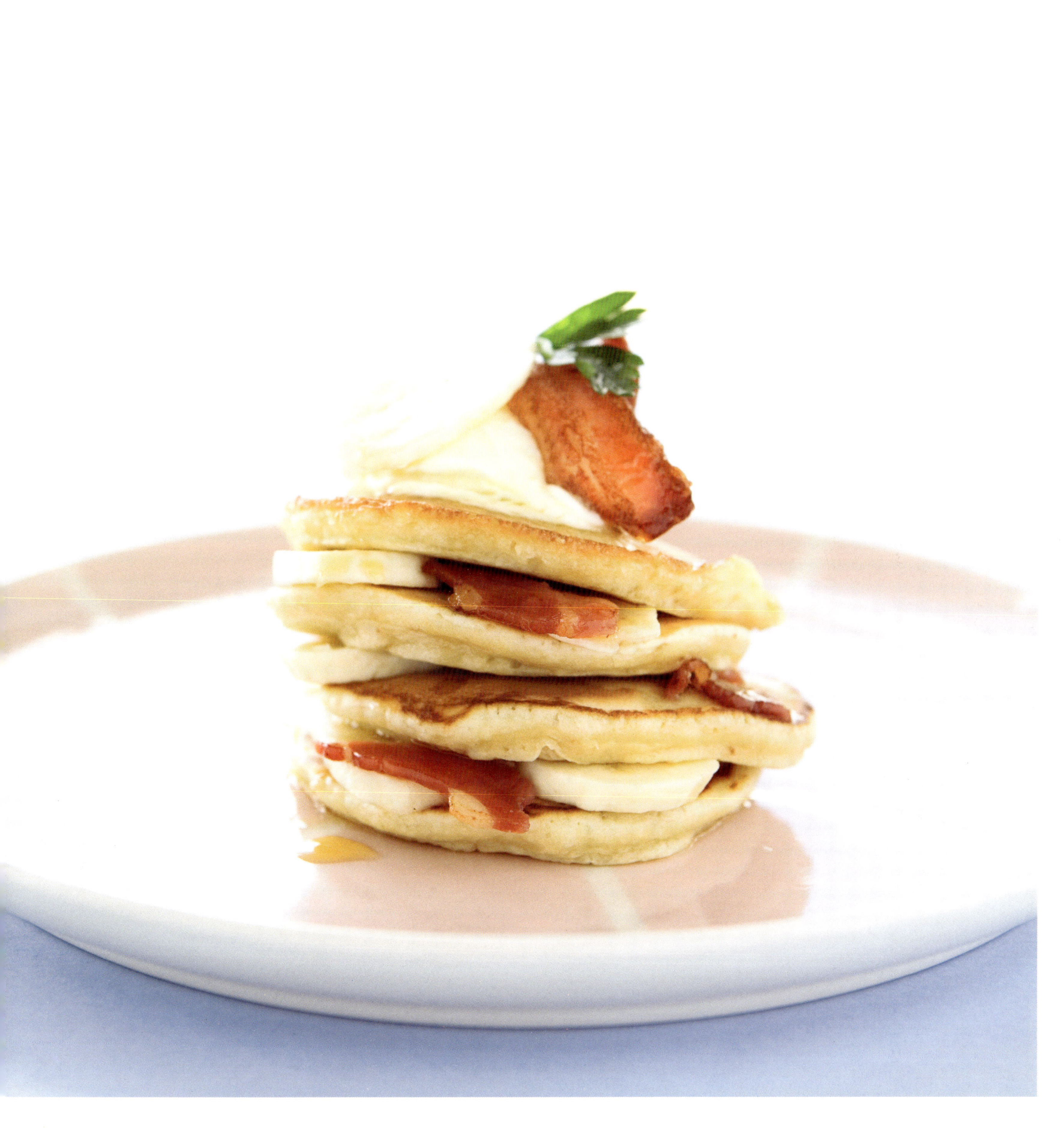

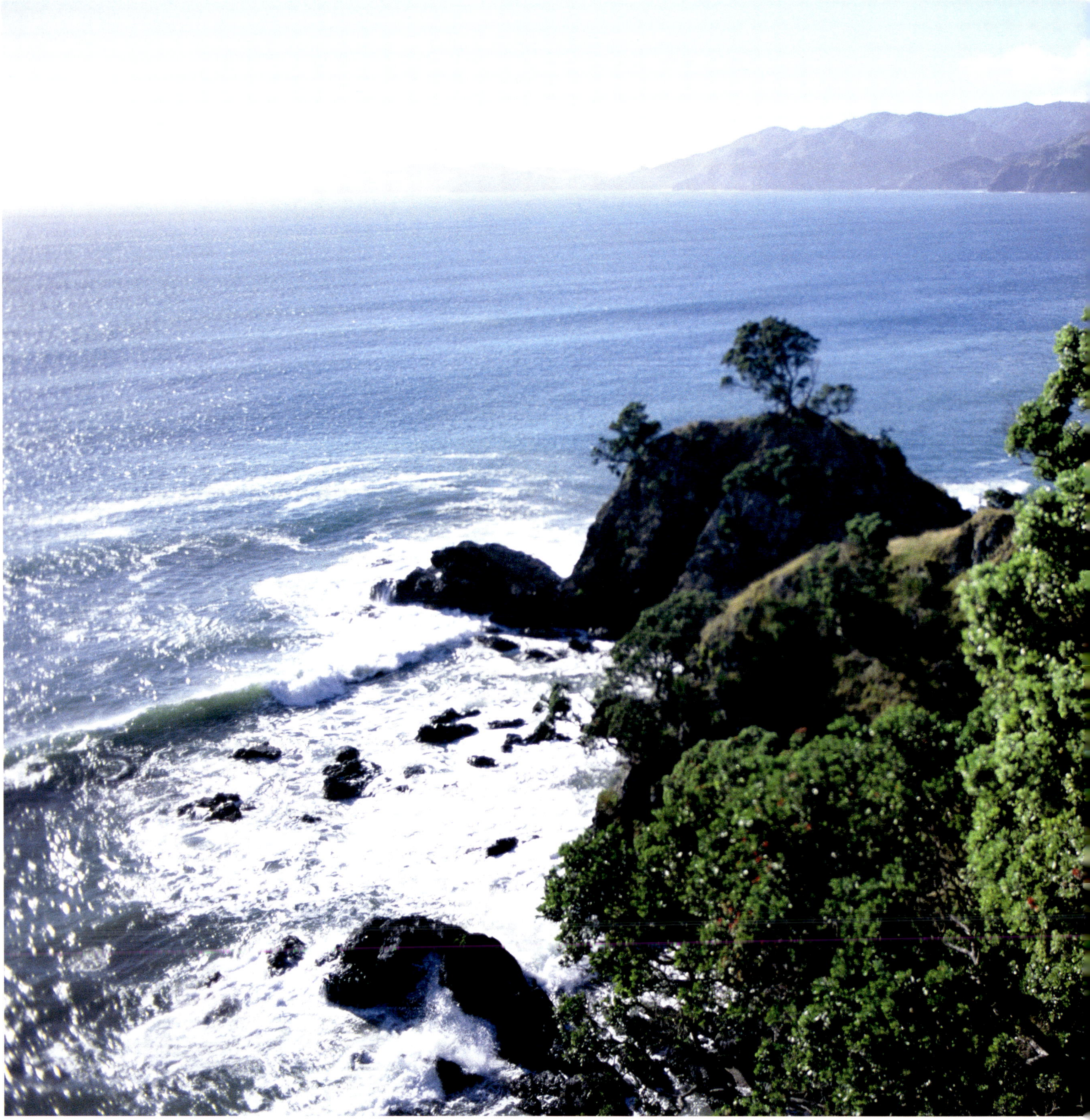

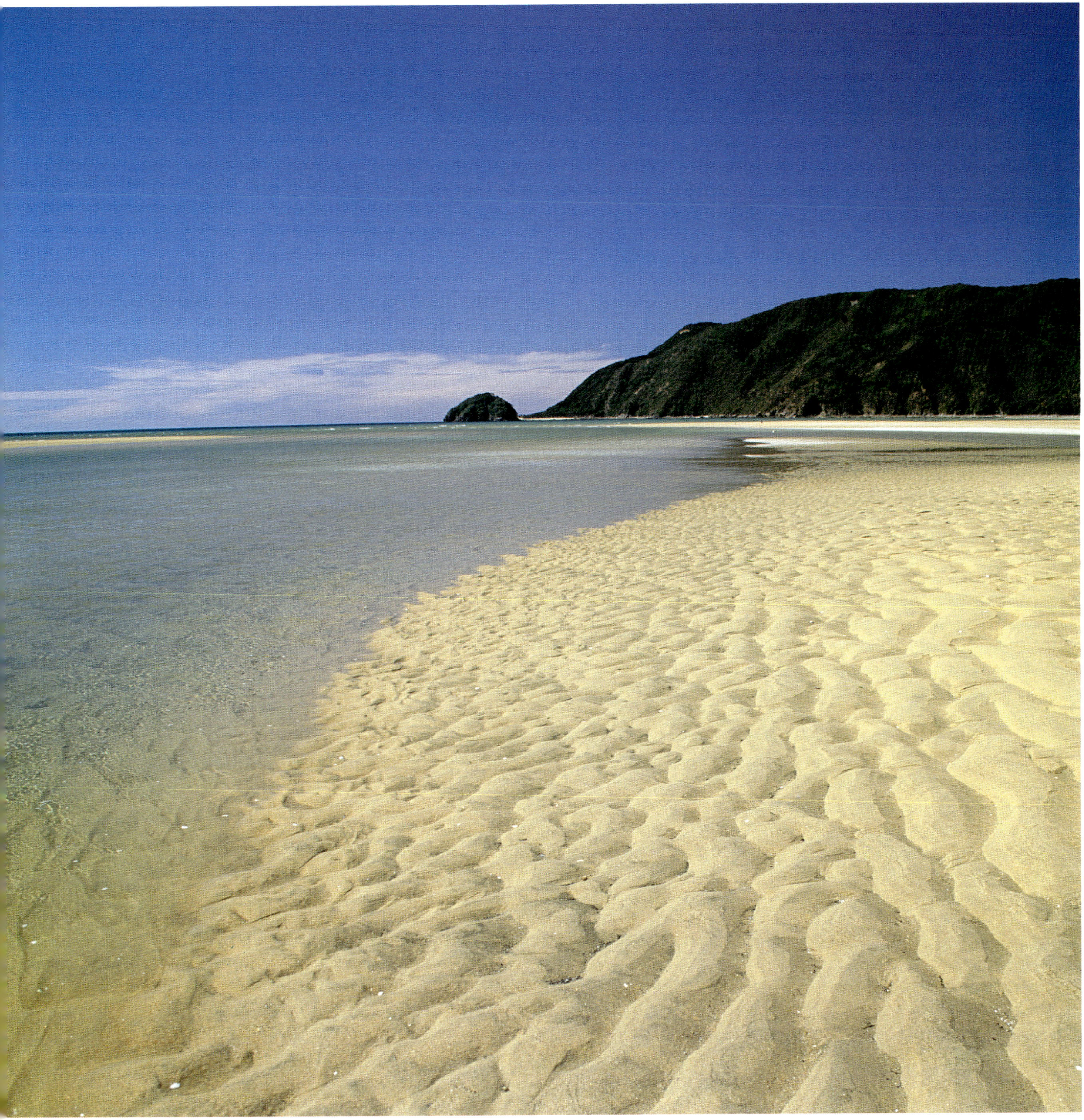

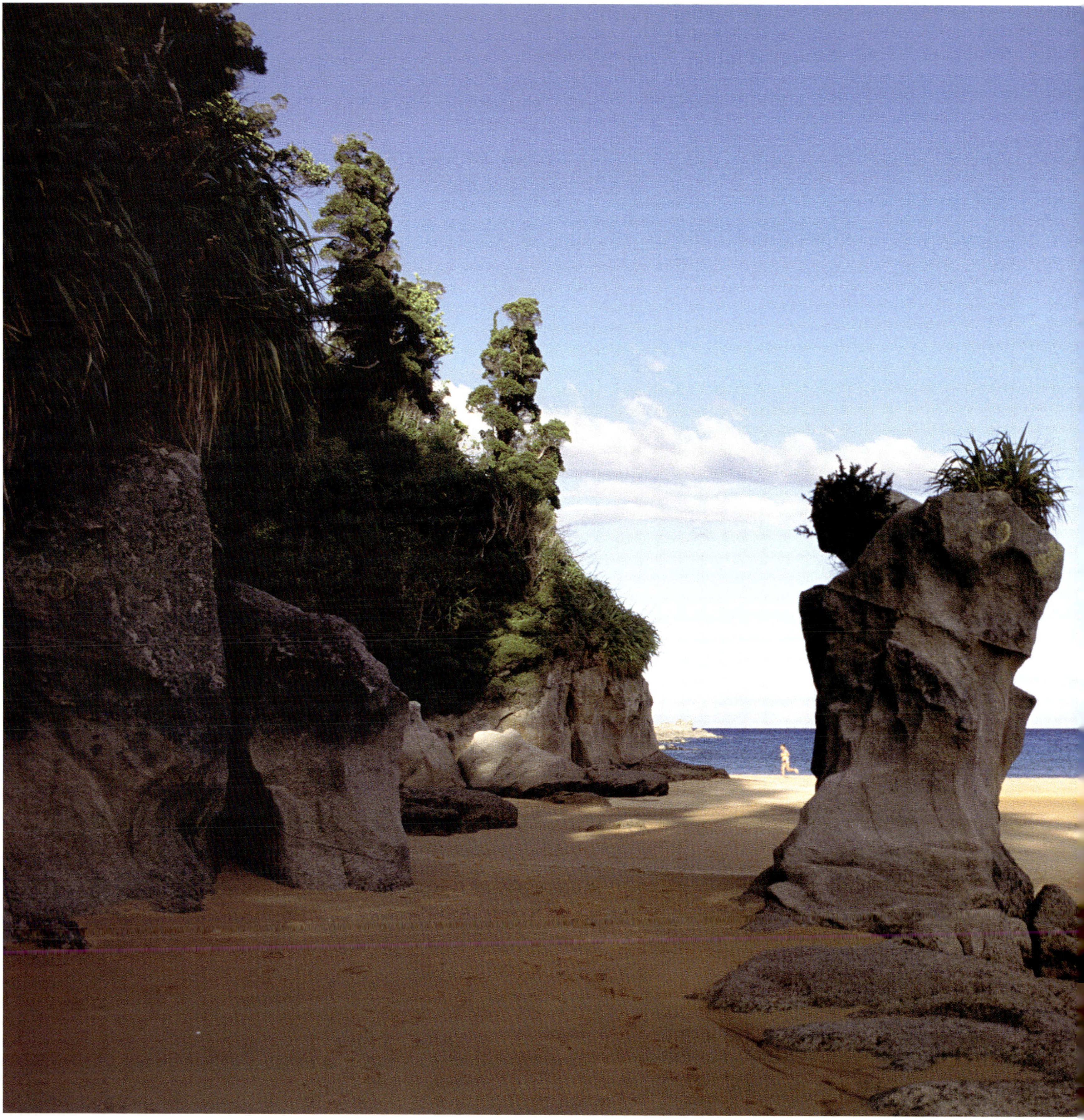

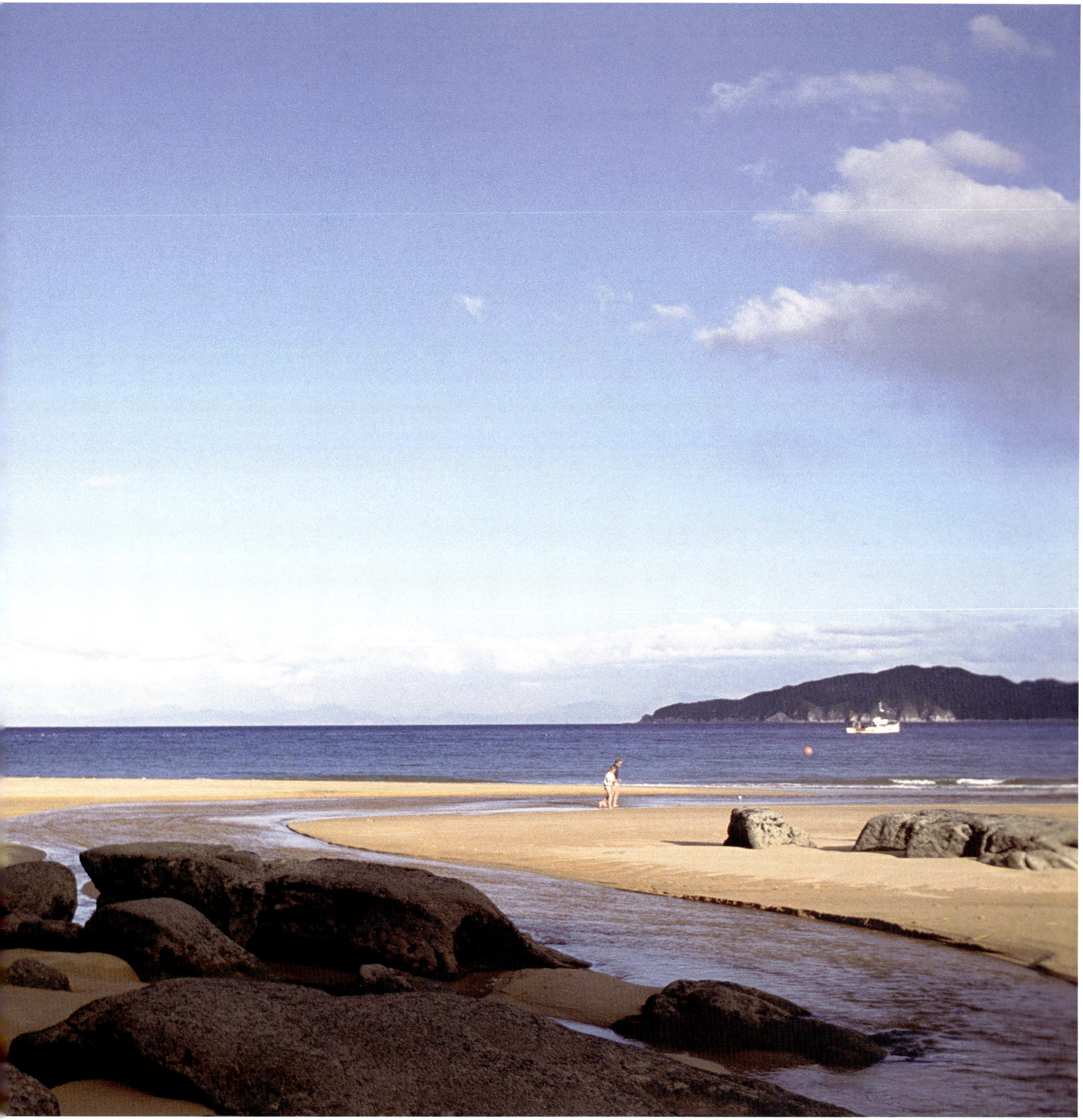

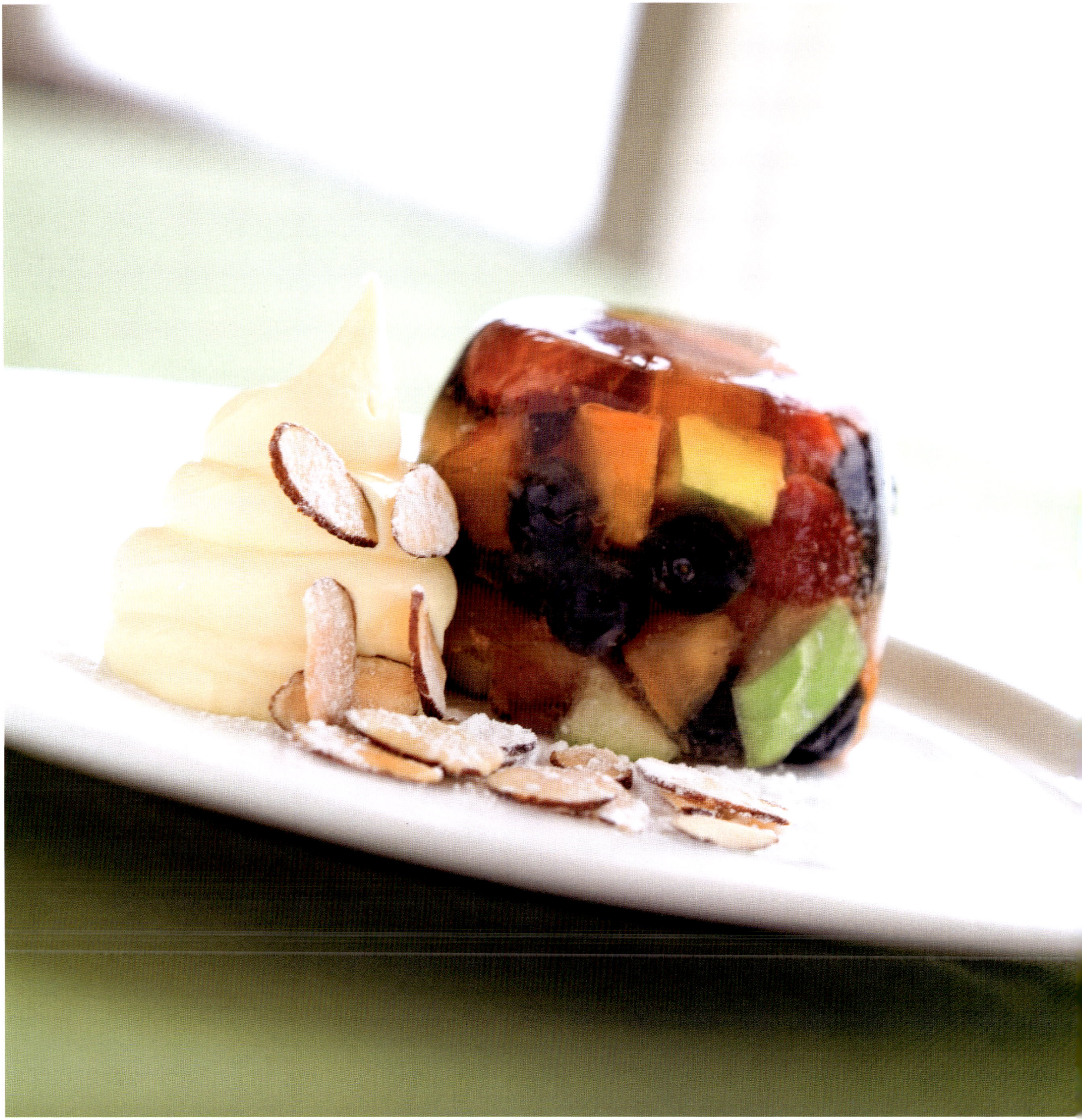

Fruit Jelly

Serves 6

Ingredients

4½ tsp gelatine powder
150 ml (⅔ cup) boiling water
500 ml (2 cups) clear apple juice
4 cups diced fresh fruit and berries
½ cup sliced almonds
300 ml (1¼ cups) cream, whipped to soft peak

Place gelatine in a bowl. Pour in boiling water and whisk briskly to dissolve.
Pour in apple juice. Mix well and set aside.
Divide fruit between 6 x 250 ml cups. Pour in apple juice mixture. Cover and refrigerate for 5 hours or until set.
Preheat oven to 200°C. Place almonds evenly on a baking tray. Cook in oven until brown.

Assembly

Dip the base of each cup in hot water for 25 seconds, then turn out onto plates.
Spoon cream beside jelly, sprinkle with almonds and dust with icing sugar.

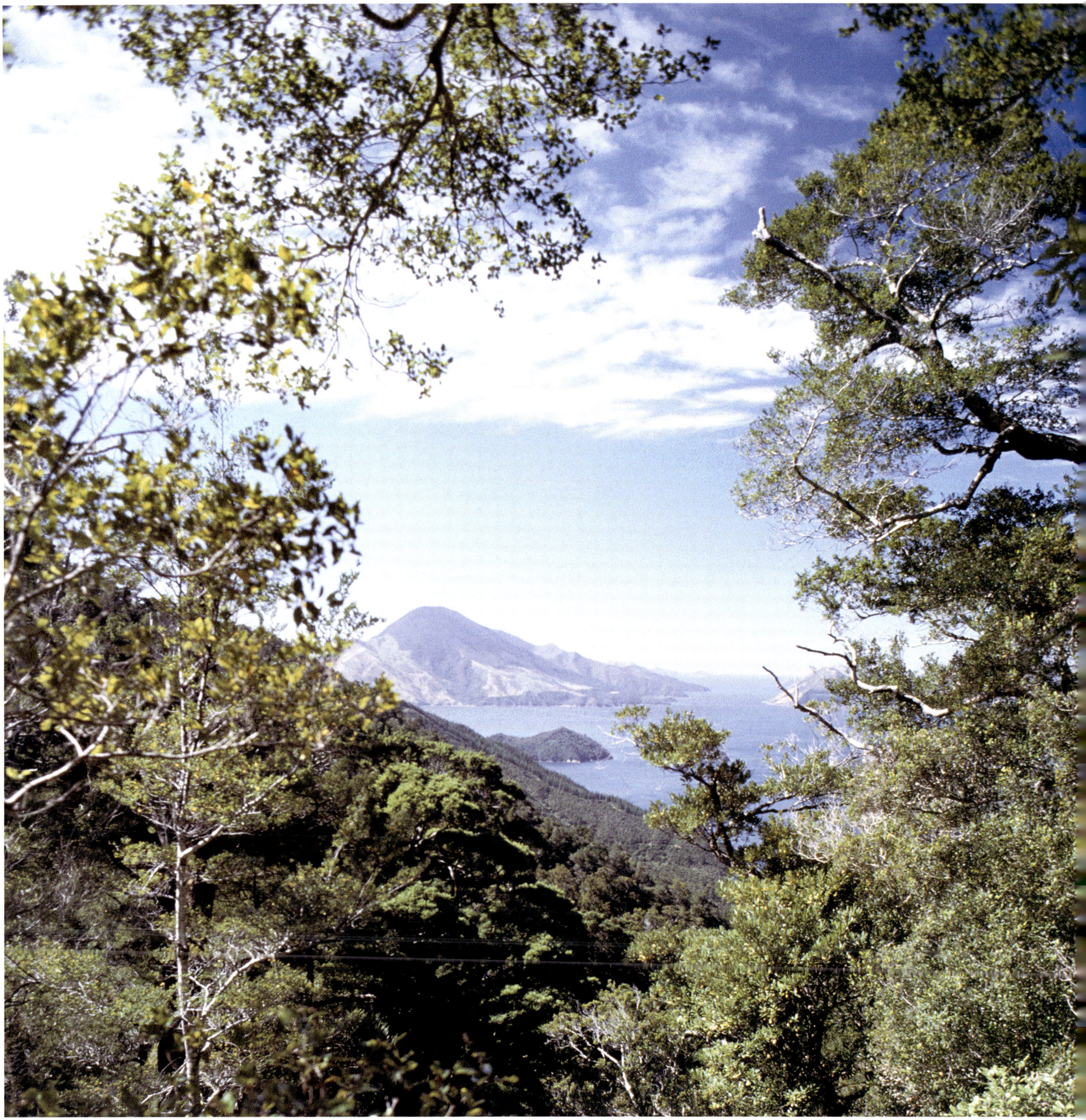

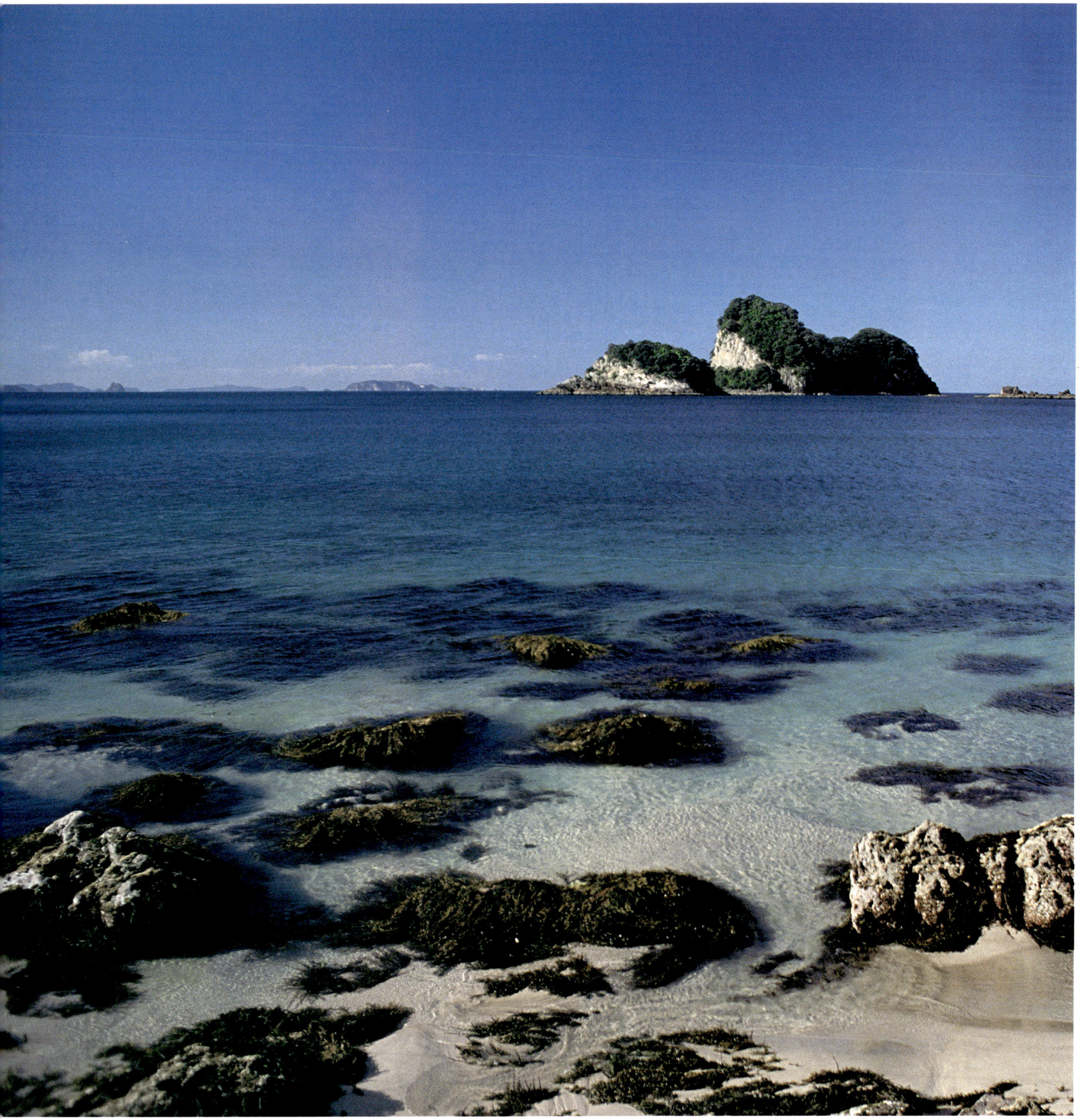

Peach Crumble with Raspberries and Vanilla Ice Cream

Serves 4

Ingredients

2 tbsp soft brown sugar
¼ cup rolled oats
¼ cup breadcrumbs
¼ cup desiccated coconut
50 g soft butter
4 peaches, halved, stones removed
1 cup fresh or frozen raspberries
4 large scoops vanilla ice cream
icing sugar for dusting

Preheat oven to 200°C.
Mix together sugar, oats, breadcrumbs and coconut. Work in butter with fingers to form a lumpy crumble. Place peach halves on a baking tray, cut side up. Top each peach half with the crumble mix. Cook for approximately 10 minutes or until the crumble mix has turned brown.

Assembly

Place 2 peach halves on each plate. Add raspberries, defrosted if necessary, and a scoop of ice cream. Dust with icing sugar and serve.

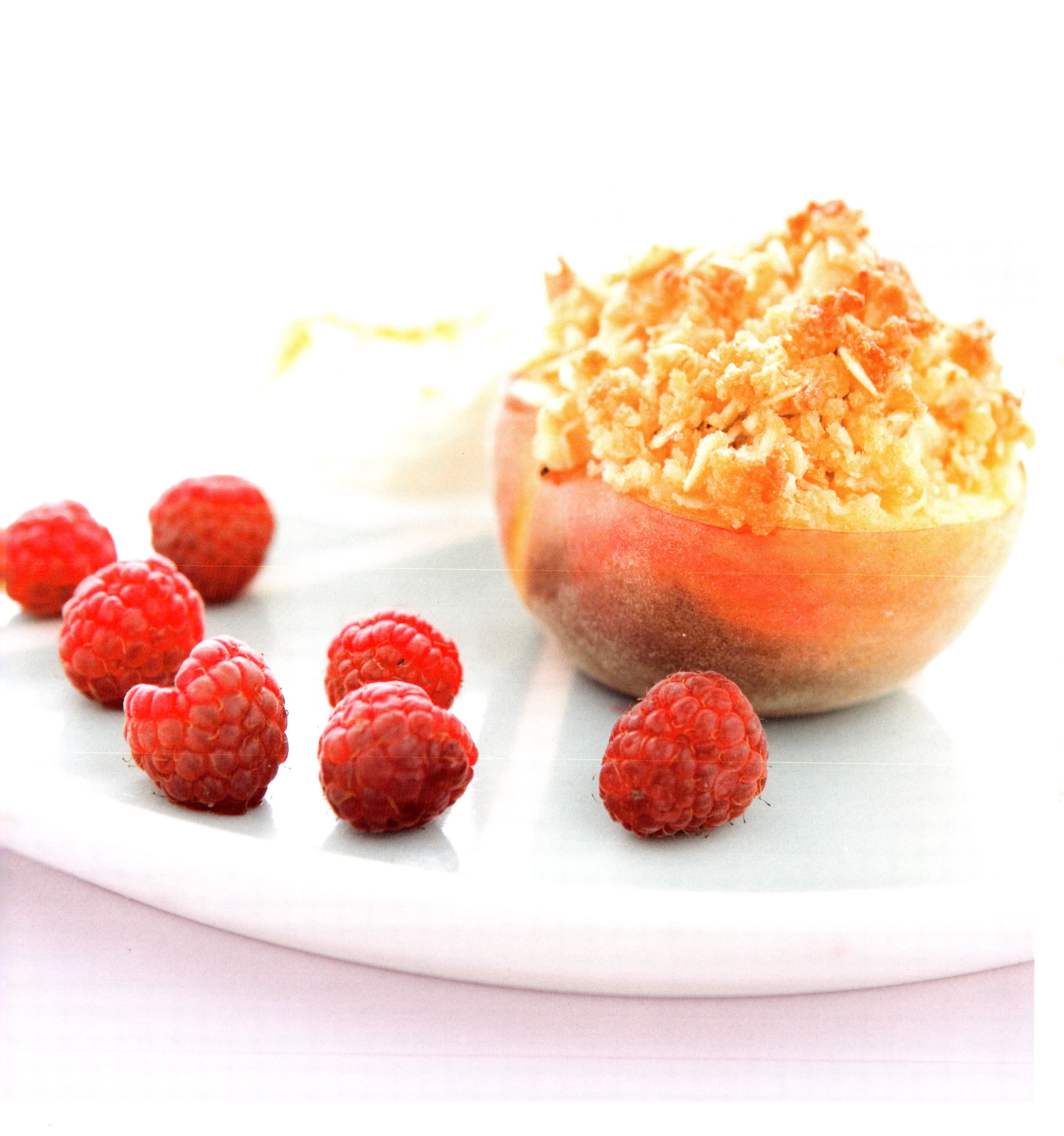

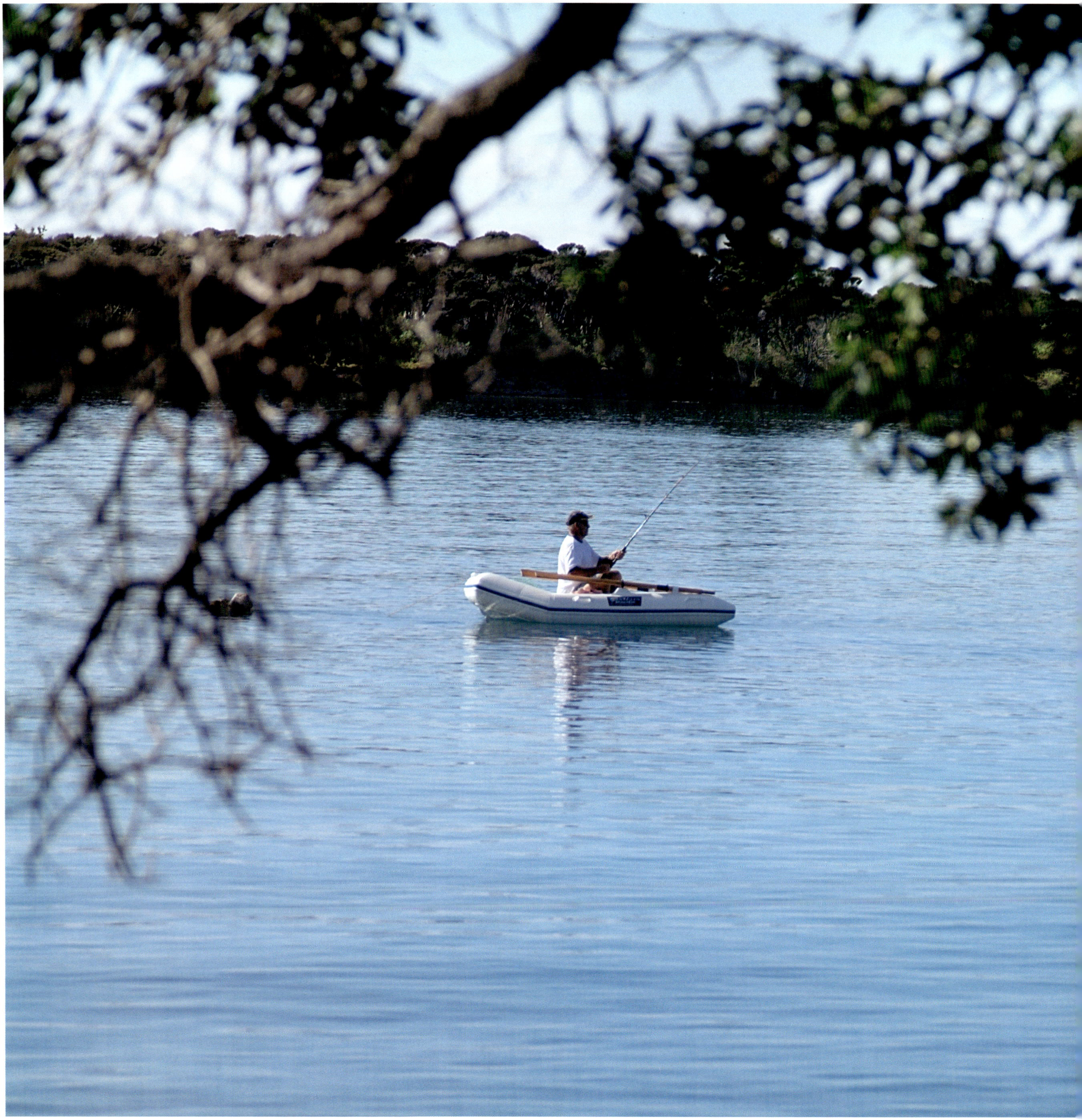

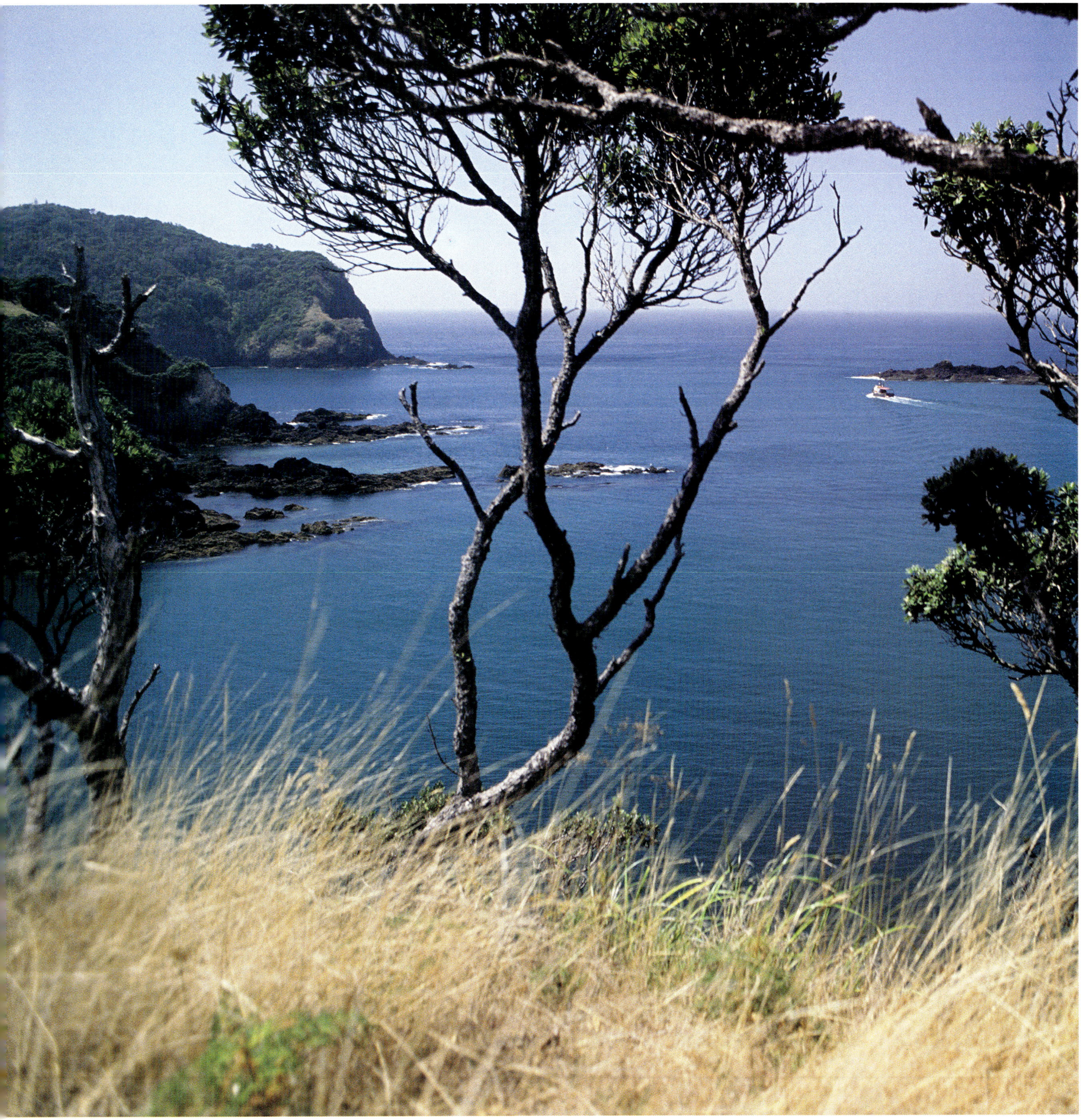

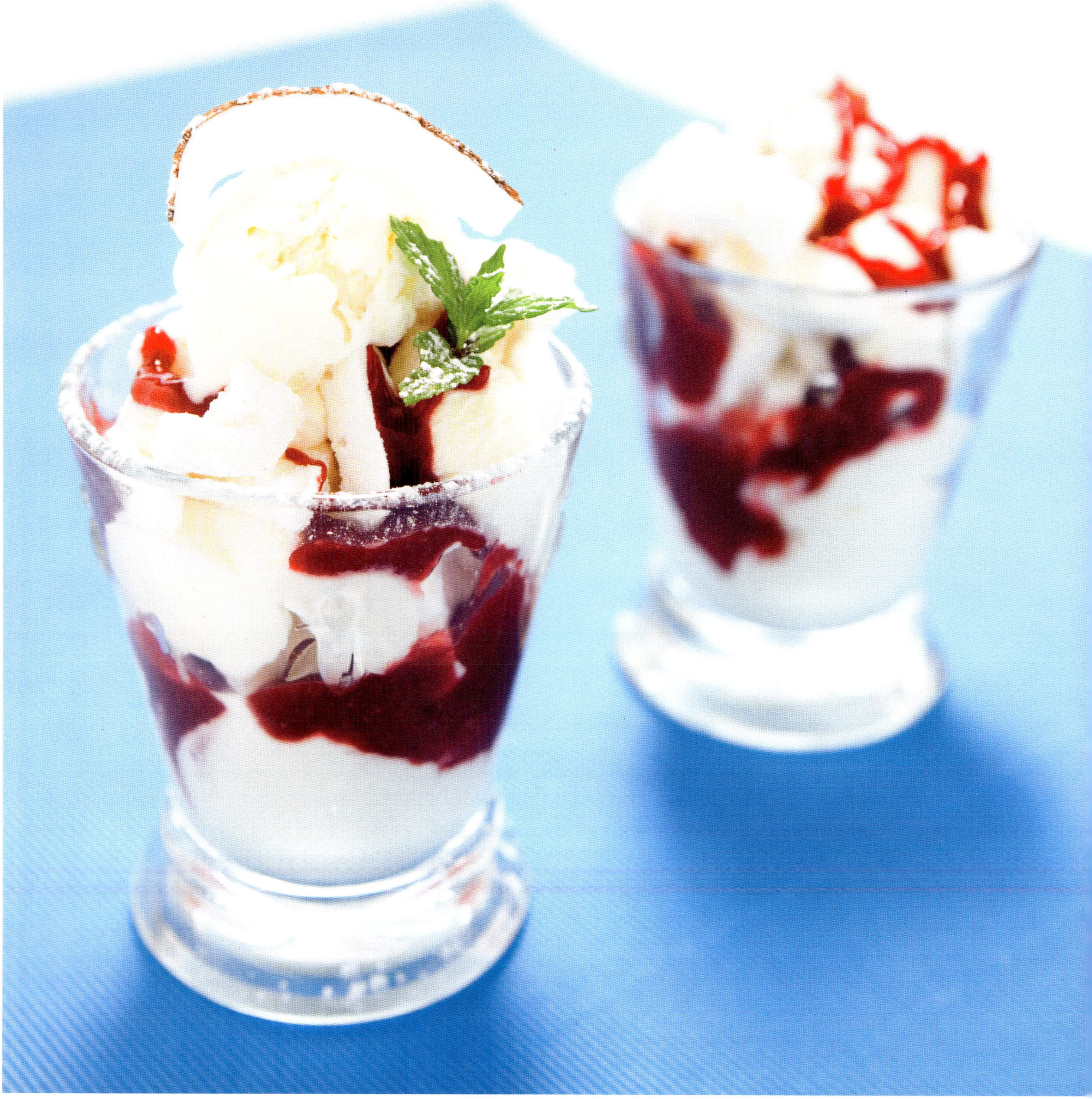

Plum, Coconut and Meringue Sundae

Serves 4

Ingredients

12 red plums, halved, stones removed
60 ml (¼ cup) sugar
2 tbsp water
300 ml (1¼ cups) cream, whipped to soft peak
12 store-bought meringues, 3 per serve
½ cup desiccated coconut, lightly toasted
8 large scoops vanilla ice cream
icing sugar for dusting

Bring plums, sugar and water to the boil. Simmer for 5 minutes or until soft, stirring occasionally. Blend until smooth or push through a sieve. Let cool.

Assembly

Assemble in individual serving glasses. Spoon 2 tbsp cream into each serving glass. Break 1 meringue into 4 pieces and push into cream. Sprinkle with 1 tbsp coconut. Place a scoop of ice cream on top. Coat with plum sauce. Tap the glass on bench to settle layers. Repeat the layering process, finishing with ice cream. Sprinkle top with coconut. Dust with icing sugar and serve.

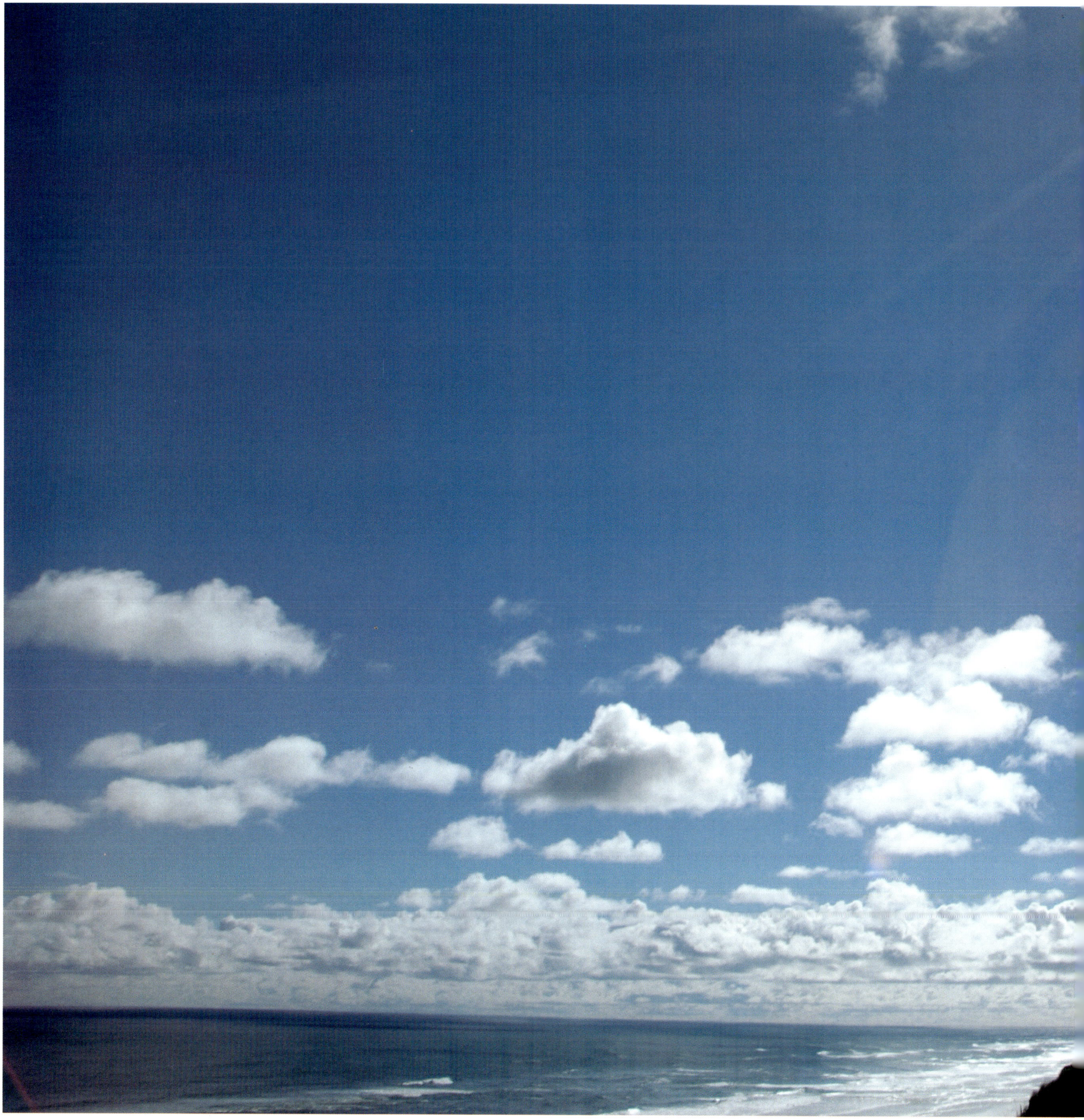

Shortbread, Lime Cream and Berries

Serves 6

Ingredients

125 g soft butter
60 g icing sugar
175 g flour
extra flour for dusting
1½ cups summer berries
   (approximately ¼ cup per serve)
mint leaves for decoration
icing sugar for dusting

Lime Cream

250 g crème fraîche
zest and juice of 1 lime
2 tbsp sugar
1 tbsp vanilla essence
250 ml (1 cup) cream, whipped to
   soft peak

Preheat oven to 170°C.
Cream butter and sugar together.
Mix in flour to form a dough.
Lightly flour work surface. Roll out dough to 1 cm thickness. Cut rounds with a large pastry cutter or a strong glass. This should make about 6 biscuits. Place rounds on a lightly greased tray and bake for approximately 25 minutes or until the biscuits are firm when touched in the middle. Meanwhile, make the Lime Cream.

To make the Lime Cream

Place crème fraîche, lime zest and juice, sugar and vanilla in a bowl and whisk together well. Add cream and mix well. Cover and refrigerate for 10 minutes.

Assembly

Place 1 biscuit on each plate. Divide Lime Cream between the 6 shortbread biscuits. Top with berries and mint. Dust with icing sugar and serve.

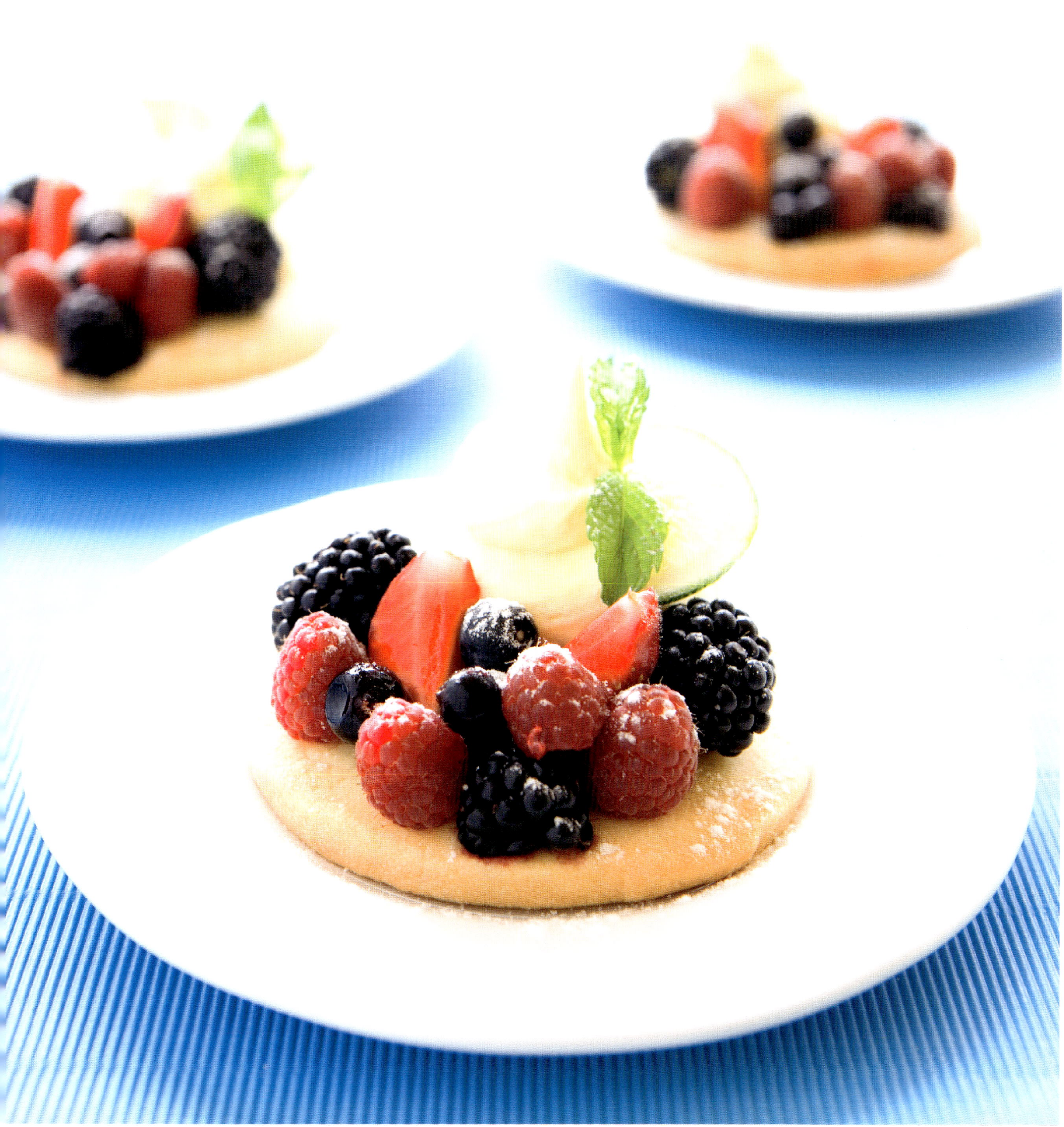